COMPETITIVE PRODUCT DEVELOPMENT

A Quality Approach to Succeeding in the 90s and Beyond

COMPETITIVE PRODUCT DEVELOPMENT

A Quality Approach to Succeeding in the 90s and Beyond

by
Rudolph G. Boznak

with
Audrey K. Decker

ASQC Quality Press
Milwaukee, Wisconsin 53202

BUSINESS ONE IRWIN
Homewood, Illinois 60430

Richard D. Irwin, Inc.:
Sponsoring editor: Jean Marie Geracie
Project editor: Ethel Shiell
Production manager: Diane Palmer
Designer: Larry J. Cope
Art coordinator: Heather Burbridge
Compositor: AppleTree Graphics
Typeface: 11/13 Palatino
Printer: Book Press

ASQC Quality Press:
Acquisitions assistant: Deborah Dunlap
Marketing administrator: Mark Olson
Acquisitions editor: Susan Westergard
Production editor: Annette Wall

Library of Congress Cataloging-in-Publication Data

Boznak, Rudolph G.
    Competitive product development : a quality approach to succeeding in the '90s and beyond / by Rudolph G. Boznak with Audrey K. Decker.
        p.   cm.
    Includes bibliographical references and index.
    ISBN 1-55623-977-7
    1. Production management—Quality control.   2. New products.
I. Decker, Audrey K.   II. Title.
TS156.B69   1993
658.5'75—dc20   92–39622

Printed in the United States of America

1 2 3 4 5 6 7 8 9 0 BP 0 9 8 7 6 5 4 3

ASQC
Quality Press
611 East Wisconsin Avenue
Milwaukee, WI 53202

This book is dedicated to our devoted companion, Heidi, who relinquished her favorite pastimes whilst we wrote this book.

Preface

Competitive product development—there's that much used C word again. Admittedly, being competitive is a much sought-after and worthy objective. But what does *being competitive* really mean? Setting all rhetoric aside, the business of business is making and selling products and services that customers either want or need to buy. *Competitiveness*, then, is simply being better at making and selling than anybody else.

Unfortunately, executives have failed to hear this subtle message. They have yet to learn that the battle for competitiveness cannot be won solely by manipulation of financial numbers, acquisition of nonrelated businesses, or development of strategic alliances. Nor is it to be found in a company's cleverness of advertising or grandness of scale. *True business competitiveness is determined by the products its customers purchase.* In essence, the marketplace is nature's way of organizing choice and casting votes. Ultimately, it is the marketplace that ascribes the level of a company's competitiveness. In this context, the company with the best product development capability wins.

If we continue this argument to its logical conclusion,

the focus of every business should be to develop products and services that provide the greatest amount of customer satisfaction. Imagine if this were the case. Given their natural resources, technological creativity, entrepreneurial spirit, and infrastructure, U.S. manufacturers should be the best product developers in the world.

Unfortunately, they're not. More leaders of smokestack products, electronics, semiconductor, automotive, and computer industries are finding themselves *less*, rather than *more*, competitive. Most are finding it more difficult to rival their international competitors. The question is, Why?

Is it because, according to Peter Drucker, too many executives believe being good at product development is "grubby detail work"? Would we rather attempt to "deal our way to success"? In this regard, Drucker offers an interesting perspective: "Dealmaking beats working. Dealmaking is exciting and fun, and working is grubby. Running anything is primarily an enormous amount of grubby detail work with very little excitement, so dealmaking is kind of romantic, sexy."[1]

I will not attempt to second-guess the intentions of management. Also, I do not believe executives are unwilling to roll up their sleeves and tackle the grubby work required to return their businesses to a more competitive track. To the contrary, many have been hard at work developing competitive strategies, expending critical resources, and operationalizing new tools and methodologies. Yet for all this effort, success has escaped them. This is not for their want of trying, but for their inability to operationalize these initiatives effectively.

This scenario reminds me of a quote in the office of a business school professor: "There is no assurance that you can keep on keeping on." Being an aviation pioneer did not ensure PanAm's survival. Technology did not ensure IBM's business base. Nor did size ensure GM's market share. Unquestionably, today's global competitive challenges provide three very personal and pertinent reasons why you should take time to experience this book.

Reason 1. A broad range of studies highlights distressing findings that the U.S.'s *ability to compete within the emerging international and global markets has seriously deteriorated.* Of particular importance are the following:

(1) New product development and cost management are continuing trouble areas for U.S. manufacturers. Studies suggest that their productivity gains are less than half those of major competitors.

(2) While most manufacturing executives *know* about the approaches necessary to compete into the 21st century, few are able to *operationalize* them effectively.

(3) There are no "quick fixes" for today's competitive issues. There are no "silver-bullet" or "turnkey" methodologies on the horizon. Competitive improvements can only be found through a renewed understanding of the basics of business—product development.

(4) New international challenges from the European Community, the Pacific Rim, and South America will significantly increase competitive pressures in the future. Tough as it may seem, competition will never be easier than it is today!

(5) Effective product development is no longer an option. New international initiatives such as ISO 9000 are mandating that manufacturers conform to verifiable product development standards *before* their products or services can be sold to international markets.

Reason 2.   To be competitive, you must increasingly entice potential customers with more high-quality, price-competitive products than your competitors do. More so, you must introduce these new products *before* your competition does. Meeting these aggressive objectives requires the presence of two critical success factors: first, an *understanding* of the principles of product development and second, an efficient product development *capability*.

Reason 3.   One of the most critical challenges facing a business leader is how to personally visualize and lead the operationalization of the right initiatives to improve your product development capability. Most organizations and functional staffs have become so inculcated in their suboptimized points of view that they need your vision and guidance to see their way forward. Only an insightful business leader can integrate the strategy and tactics necessary to responsively transition their business into a more competitive new product development paradigm.

Thus, the purpose of this book is not to provide you with a recipe solution but with insight, distilled principles, and business examples. It will challenge your corporate mind-set and enable you to better visualize your product development environment. It is your pragmatic guide to analyze and revitalize your approach to product development. Finally, its message can empower your product development processes to develop and introduce new products faster, more reliably, and at less cost than your competitors.

Rudolph G. Boznak
Audrey K. Decker

Acknowledgments

Special thanks to:

- Audrey Kay Decker for her creativity in brain-storming the paradigm with me, her relentless research and her ability to help state these ideas in a comprehensible manner.

- Mark Douglas Decker for providing continuous support over the last 10 years and being a best friend.

- The membership of professional societies, who have challenged and debated these concepts in their quest and promotion of excellence. Without you, there would be no yardstick of measure. Thank you:

> American Society for Quality Control
>
> Project Management Institute
>
> American Production and Inventory Control Society
>
> Institute of Industrial Engineering
>
> American Society of Mechanical Engineers

American Society for Engineering Management

Institute of Electrical and Electronic Engineers

American Defense Preparedness Association

American Association of Cost Engineers

American Management Association

- Our parents, Annabel and Rudolph Boznak and Bernie and Carl Decker, who lovingly gave us the opportunity to experience each other and this adventure called life.

NOTE

This book contains a number of references to companies and people. In the context that these references exemplify approaches and views, they should in no way be construed as a judgment of good or bad business practice. The author has diligently tried to ensure that the facts in these cases are correct, or were correct at the time of the research, and has attempted to give maximum credit to facts published by others. Any opinions one may draw from the book are strictly the authors', and have no reflection of the opinions of previous employers or clients.

R.G.B.
A.K.D.

Contents

List of Figures   xvii

1   INTRODUCTION: COMPETITIVE PRODUCT
     DEVELOPMENT: A CALL FOR ACTION   1
     Competitive Product Development: A Call for Action, 3
     Mastering Product Development Management:
     A New Premise, 8
     Three Tenets of Effective Product Development, 11
     Carpe Diem (Seize the Day), 17

2   DEPROGRAMMING YOUR
     SUBCONSCIOUS   19
     The Subconscious Management Influence, 20
     Vitalism, Atomism, and Product Development, 22
     The Japanese Approach, 25
     The U.S. Approach, 26

3   MUSUBI: UNLOCKING THE POWER OF
     YOUR MIND   28
     The Art of Visualization, 29
     Balance, 30

Harmonious Unification, 32

Oneness, 35

4   DISCERNING THE PAST: THE SOURCE OF
     TODAY'S PROBLEMS   38
     The Nature of Work, 39
     Pragmatism and Paradigms, 42
     Institutionalized Product Development Inadequacies, 54

5   THE RESULTS OF REALITY: A NEW
     PARADIGM EMERGES   57
     A Time for Action, 59
     A New Paradigm Emerges, 61

6   OPERATIONALIZING THE NEW
     PARADIGM   69
     Product Development Management Principles, 71
     Communicating the *It*, 73
     Product Development: The Process, 76
     Managing the Organizational Elements, 84

7   ASSURING PROCESS STABILITY   88
     The Source of Stability, 88
     The Product Definition Process, 90
     Organizational Stability and the Product Development
     Process, 100
     Building Stability into the Product Development
     Process, 101

8   EFFECTIVELY MANAGING PRODUCT
     CHANGE   113
     Two Change Management Myths, 114
     Do You Have a Change Management Problem? 120
     Managing versus Administering Change, 124
     Screening Change Requests, 127
     Business/Product Intelligence, 131
     Actioning and Communicating a Change Request, 133
     Expediting the Change Process, 134

The Elements of Change Management, 135

Compressing Change Management, 136

Evaluating Cost Management of Change Control, 139

Evaluating the Change Management Operating
System, 140

Change Management and Organizational Learning, 143

9   PRODUCT INTEGRITY AND CUSTOMER
     SATISFACTION   144

Change Incorporation, 146

Change Incorporation versus Effectivity, 147

Analyzing Your Incorporation Process, 151

PDM: An International Issue, 156

10   ENERGIZING YOUR ORGANIZATION FOR
     ACTION   161

Barriers to Change, 162

The Change Process: Overcoming Change Barriers, 164

The New Paradigm and the Change Process, 167

The Quest for Competitiveness, 170

Endnotes   175

Index   177

List of Figures

CHAPTER 1

Figure 1–1   United States, Japan, and West German
              Product Development   5

CHAPTER 2

Figure 2–1   U.S./Japanese Product Development
              Comparison Model   25

Figure 2–2   Japanese Approach to Product Development
              Initiatives   26

Figure 2–3   U.S. Approach to Product Development Initiatives   27

CHAPTER 3

Figure 3–1   The Art of Visualization   30

CHAPTER 4

Figure 4–1   The Nature of Work   39

Figure 4–2   The Nature of Productivity Influence   41

Figure 4–3   Mean Expenditures for Primary Product
              Development Phases   41

Figure 4–4   Timing of Product Definition Achievement   43

Figure 4–5   "We'll-Know-It-When-We-See-It" Case Example   44

Figure 4–6   Creating Plateaus of Stability   46

Figure 4–7   Case Example: Product Development
              Management Dynamics   47

Figure 4–8   Stability and Cycle Compression Opportunities   48
Figure 4–9   Accelerated Time-to-Margin Contribution   50
Figure 4–10   Achieving Product Reliability, Maintainability, and
              Quality Targets   51
Figure 4–11   Containing Product Development Costs   53

CHAPTER 5

Figure 5–1   Today's Product Development Paradigm   58
Figure 5–2   The Competitive Product Development Paradigm   62
Figure 5–3   Examples of Perceived Feature Values   66

CHAPTER 6

Figure 6–1   New Product Development: A Structured Process   77
Figure 6–2   New Product Development:
              Opposing Perspectives   78
Figure 6–3   Channelling New Product Development Creativity   80
Figure 6–4   Critical New Product Development
              Decision Points   82
Figure 6–5   Integrating the Princples and the Process   83
Figure 6–6   The Benefits of Right-First-Time Development
              and Operations   85

CHAPTER 7

Figure 7–1   Dependent and Independent Zones   104
Figure 7–2   The Dynamics of Dependent Change   105
Figure 7–3   Creating Autonomous Design Zones   108
Figure 7–4   Results of Uncontrolled Early Project Loading   109

CHAPTER 8

Figure 8–1   Case Study Example: Controlling
              Continuous Improvement   119
Figure 8–2   Completing the Periodicity Profile   123
Figure 8–3   Change Screening Opportunities   128
Figure 8–4   The First Screen: Reduce the Number of Requests   129
Figure 8–5   The Second Screen: Reduce the Disruptive Effects   130
Figure 8–6   The Third Screen: Reduce the Time to
              Action a Change   137

Chapter One

Competitive Product Development: A Call for Action

E ffective product development—the ability to beat the competition in introducing reliable, cost-effective, and innovative new products and services to satisfy marketplace demand—will be the key challenge for corporate competitiveness and growth throughout the 1990s. A study of U.S. manufacturing strategy for the 1990s indicates that most executives are already putting initiatives in place to achieve effective product development.[2] The relative importance corporate executives assign to these strategic initiatives is identified by their respective ranking:

- Improve conformance quality.
- Improve vendor quality.
- Reduce unit costs.

- Reduce overhead costs.
- Reduce product development cycles.

While the intentions of U.S. manufacturers may have been headed in the right direction, the results have been perplexing. On the one hand, manufacturers have achieved significant improvement in conformance quality and overhead cost reduction. On the other hand, "U.S. companies are slowest in improving two areas where they are furthest behind. These are reducing product cost and compressing product development time."[3]

Admittedly, quality and overhead cost management are important issues. However, there are also compelling reasons why additional effort must be directed toward time-based and unit-cost competition. One reason is the continued emphasis by business strategists on a wide range of product options and lower price as differentiating competitive factors. By its very nature, this strategy requires rapid and economical development of multiple new products. Weakness in a company's ability to achieve these objectives can present an easily exploitable Achilles' heel. Containment of this potential vulnerability increases the strategic importance of possessing an effective new product development capability.

The study mentioned above concludes that while manufacturing executives may intellectually know the approaches essential to achieving best-in-class product development results, few of them fully understand the nuances of integrating and managing these technologies. Therefore, "real improvements in manufacturing competitiveness can only come through a renewed focus on the basics."[4]

Too often, business executives take comfort in the fact that most of their peers are in the same boat. However, we should not ignore the fact that this message has another perspective. Read it again, with the following emphasis: While most manufacturing executives may intellectually *know* the approaches essential to achieving best-in-class product development results, *a few of them fully understand the nuances of integrating and managing these technologies.* Unfortunately, if you're not in this category, then these few are your competitors!

If one measures the truth of these findings by comparing domestic productivity improvement against that of major competitors, America is not doing well. In fact, the U.S. manufacturing productivity trend is quite disturbing. For example, the 1988 and 1989 average annual productivity growth among Japanese manufacturers was 5.2 percent, and the United Kingdom did as well; France's productivity spurted at a 4.9 percent pace, and West Germany's rose by 4.5 percent. But in that same two-year period, U.S. manufacturing productivity grew at a meager annual rate of 2.1 percent—despite the emphasis on improving competitiveness.[5] This suggests that perhaps too many companies are still doing business as usual.

COMPETITIVE PRODUCT DEVELOPMENT: A CALL FOR ACTION

There are two truths about the element of time: (1) It is a precious resource, and (2) It is seldom on your side. Companies have found these truths especially relevant whenever they have attempted to operationalize new product development initiatives. The inability to responsively achieve aggressive product development objectives (compressed development time, reduced cost, and improved quality) has caused many businesses to be overrun by very formidable and growing competitive sources.

The examples are all around us. The United States is

losing its leadership in the automotive sector. The computer industry is under heavy attack, and consumer electronics manufacturing is essentially gone. Who are the challengers to your competitiveness, and where should your near-term concerns be focused? The first and most widely publicized, debated, and copied competitive force is obviously the Japanese manufacturing and quality phenomenon. However, you must be aware of several others as well.

The European Community

A less verbalized, yet potentially contending, force than Japan is the increasingly cohesive European Community (EC). The full implications of European unification could extend beyond the original EC membership to encompass the vast markets of Russia and the other former Soviet republics. The emerging "Fortress Europe" being shaped, more by economics than by politics, offers greater market challenges to U.S. industries than those offered by Japan.

A primary reason is that "during the past five years, major Japanese corporations have doubled their direct investments in the European Community. Japan now produces more in Europe than it exports to Europe, a trend that will most likely continue. The result is, while Europe will be a major source of earnings for Japan, Japan will not reciprocate as a major importer of EC manufactured goods."[6] Hence, a scenario is being cast for a potential tightening of competitive trade options between the EC and non-EC countries. This may not be because of choice, but because of economic and political survival.

The EC's strategy of increasing internal integration also poses several challenges that strike at the very heart of the United States' industrial capability. One is the EC's goal to improve advanced microelectronics, electronics, software and information technologies, and computer-integrated-

FIGURE 1–1
**United States, Japan, and West German Product
Development**

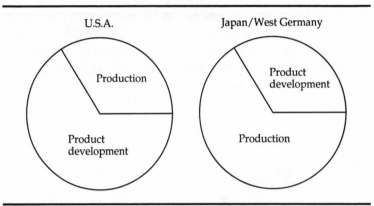

manufacturing competitiveness. These are targets frighteningly similar to those of U.S. businesses.

To achieve these objectives, the EC strategy emphasizes applied research—one of the U.S.'s weakest product development areas. Figure 1–1 illustrates this gap between West Germany, Japan, and the United States.

Here, studies show that "U.S. companies typically expend two thirds of their effort developing a product and one third on production techniques. Whereas, Japanese and West German firms reverse the ratios."[7]

In essence, it takes a U.S. manufacturer twice as long to conceptualize and commercialize a new product as it takes its major competitors. This approach not only penalizes U.S. product development capability but may also prevent the United States from achieving greater economic manufacturing cost and quality benefits.

Another challenge is the EC's efforts to collectively address ways to improve its manufacturing capabilities. The purpose is to offset competitive advantages of countries with lower labor costs or higher levels of automation. Success of these initiatives will make U.S. manufacturing-based competitiveness much more difficult to sustain in the future.

The political challenges of the EC have caused some to doubt its threat. However, the fall of the Berlin Wall and the demise of communism in Europe have greatly increased the EC's global potential. The abundance and proximity of talented and eager Eastern European scientists, engineers, programmers, and technicians bring the EC's seemingly long-range objectives into much closer view.

Southeast Asia

Southeast Asia also poses a growing threat, one "that is financed by more than $50 billion of foreign investment commitments over the next five years. Japan, now the largest shareholder of the Asian Development Bank, funds more than 90 percent of the bank's soft loan portfolio. Needless to say, 9 of the top 10 recipient countries are in Asia."[8]

A projected outcome of this funding trend can be extrapolated from the strategy adopted by the government of Malaysia. "Prime Minister Mahathir bin Mohamad promotes a 'Look East' policy and says bluntly that his nation intends to become an industrial power by emulating Japan, not America. Mahathir has proposed an Asian trade bloc that would include Japan but exclude the United States."[9]

Mexico and South America

Perhaps the least likely competitive force is the U.S.'s southern neighbors. "With the pending passage of increased free-trade agreements, Mexico can quickly become a significant force in intermediate manufactured goods and electronics."[10] Under Japan's increasing tutelage, Mexico can rapidly transform an available labor pool into a highly capable, low-cost manufacturing capability with immediate access to U.S. borders. Mexico's new president, Carlos Salinas, is taking no chances; he's already sending his children to Japanese schools.

The same sentiments are sweeping further to the south. A 1990 poll revealed that "70 percent of South Americans favored more Japanese investment. In the same survey, America placed below Romania as the last of seven (economic assistance) choices."[11]

International Standards

Finally, a more subtle and lesser-known force is the global adoption of international competitive standards such as ISO 9000. To date, "The ISO 9000 standards have been endorsed without change in the national standards sets of 53 countries. In the United States, they've been adopted as the ANSI/ASQC Q90 series. Work is also under way on the 1996 editions, in which greater changes and added requirements are expected."[12] The impact of these actions will be profound. For example, beginning January 1992, international manufacturers must have their design, development, production, test, final inspection, installation, and service processes audited and verified by an independent third party registered by the ISO committee.

The purpose of the verification process is to assure the following:

- That every product's documentation accurately and consistently matches its evolution throughout each development stage.

- That each succeeding product equals the preceding one.

- That the organization has *demonstrated the capability* to produce a quality product.

This "simple-to-say, difficult-to-do" requirement represents a major obstacle to many manufacturers. For example, all ISO 9000 signatories will give buying preference to ISO 9000 certified companies. Others will refuse to buy from noncertified businesses. This is a clear message. Failure to comply with the provisions of this standard could jeopardize an organization's international trade options. Yet, according to a recent report in *The Wall Street Journal* "only 8 percent of midsize U.S. firms plan to become certified by the end of 1992. Furthermore, only 11 percent said that they thought the standards would affect them 'a great deal' and 48 percent hadn't heard of ISO 9000."[13]

MASTERING PRODUCT DEVELOPMENT MANAGEMENT: A NEW PREMISE

Competitive forces in Japan, Europe, Mexico and South America, and Southeast Asia pose serious challenges to U.S. competitiveness, prestige, and ranking as a major economic power of the future. The repercussions are both serious and many. "If nations increasingly look to Tokyo instead of Washington for inspiration, education, goods, services, and capital, and if economic strength supplants military prowess as the main determinant of world power, the result will be a dramatic erosion of American economic and political influence."[14]

These findings are not new. Their challenges dominate our headlines and contemporary political and business thought. However, while media exhortations are important to capture our attention, they have fallen short of stating how to do what must be done. A new premise is needed, one that recognizes business executives are frustrated. They are tired of endless comparisons of how they fare against their competitors' quality, cost, and cycle compression initiatives. Instead of acrimony, executives need to know the following:

- How to quickly achieve better cost, timing, and quality performance.

- How to select appropriate strategic and tactical product development initiatives that are *right* for *their* business.

- How to operationalize these initiatives more effectively.

In essence, today's issues are not about the past; they are about the future. In the words of the legendary augur Nostradamus, the future is inevitable only if we choose to make it so. While he correctly foretold many events, Nostradamus also believed that informed and purposeful men could change the future. Similarly, the keys to overcoming your imminent, wealth-threatening competitive challenges are *knowledge* and *action*.

Admittedly, some attempts to operationalize competitive initiatives may not have yielded the desired results. Still, they have provided many of the basic tools and experiences required for success. Some have done much of the "grubby work." Now, like a sophisticated new aircraft being taxied onto the runway, these businesses are ready for takeoff. All that is needed is a qualified pilot—an astute integrator of knowledge and practice.

However, desiring to be competitive is one thing, and achieving competitiveness is quite another. Most executives can intellectually articulate competitive issues, whereas only an enlightened "integrator" can guide the dramatic improvements necessary to develop and produce higher-quality, lower-cost products faster than ever before.

What is the price for this competitive renaissance? The requirements are as simple to articulate as they are difficult to implement. They are an open and inquisitive mind, an ability to visualize, a genuine willingness to change, and an acceptance of a new role—to be the *integrator* of knowledge and practice.

Today, many businesses are at a crossroads, a juncture where the penchant for deal-making prowess embraced in the 1980s must give way to a new leadership philosophy—a personal leadership that is born of insight, understanding, and a judicious application of product development principles. To be successful, the competitive executive of the 1990s must focus less on *massaging* "the numbers" and more on *visualizing* how the numbers are really generated.

Sun Tzu's treatise *The Art of War*, written more than 2,000 years ago, provides several reasons why greater insight and understanding continue to be such critical factors for success.[15] In simple and understated brilliance, Sun Tzu states a timeless strategy for success:

- Know the enemy and know yourself; in a hundred battles you will never be in peril.

- When you are ignorant of the enemy but know yourself, your chances of winning or losing are equal.

- If ignorant both of your enemy and of yourself, you are certain in every battle to be in peril.

Sun Tzu's wisdom still rings true. It defines a strategy subscribed by three categories of rivals: the *dominator*, the *competitor*, and the *loser*. This becomes more clear when we use artistic license to exchange the words *competitor* and *customer* for the word *enemy*.

(1) Dominators: When winning is the preferred option.
Know your competitors, know your customers, and know yourself; in a hundred trials you will never be in peril.

(2) Competitors: When winning as many as you lose is an acceptable option.
When you are ignorant of your competitors and your customers but know yourself, your chances of winning or losing are equal.

(3) Losers: When winning is no longer possible.
If ignorant of your competitors, your customers, and yourself, you are certain in every trial to be in peril.

In essence, the more you understand your competitors, your customers, and yourself, the more you will avoid peril. We can only wonder what might have been, had U.S. carmakers heeded Sun Tzu's words in the 1970s, 1980s, and even into the 1990s. Perhaps they would not have so unknowingly offered the gauntlet to the Japanese in saying, "We're playing on an uneven field. Come over here and play by our rules. Then we'll see how good you really are." We know too well the rest of the story. The transplants came. They're playing on the same field and are slowly overtaking U.S. domestic car sales.

THREE TENETS OF EFFECTIVE PRODUCT DEVELOPMENT

Changing your company's competitive future will rely on your mastery of the three tenets "plagiarized" above from Sun Tzu's teachings: Know your competitors, know your product development capability, and act precisely and decisively. Together, these tenets form the thread that knits together the ideas presented in this book.

One: Know Your Competitors

Most of us learn by studying and applying the thoughts and works of others. We solve problems by experimenting with these learned formulas, principles, and techniques. However, one key source of knowledge eludes most of us—learning from our competitors. This is partly because we each tend to think and act egocentrically. We fall victim to the "I know best" syndrome.

Another reason knowledge of our competitors eludes us is we're programmed to think too small (atomically, to be exact). This creates a tendency to focus on one business issue at a time. We also tend to seek excellence by searching for "what" and "how" solutions. Initiatives such as benchmarking, reverse engineering, and competitive analysis are examples of this type of quest. Chapter Two, Deprogramming Your Subconscious, uniquely examines Eastern and Western learning approaches to reveal how each subconsciously affects today's product development methodologies.

While "what" and "how" criteria are important, you also must seek the "why" and the "when" as well. This requires that you understand not only your own business fundamentals but also the motivations underlying the obvious performance indices of your competitors. There is a term for this holistic approach: *musubi*, the principle of balance and unity, the art of harmonious unification. Chapter Three, *Musubi:* Unlocking the Power of Your Mind, unlocks your ability to read between the lines to uncover hidden factors influencing a rival's performance. More important, the principles of *musubi* can enable you to more accurately compare and effectively apply competitor practices to your product development processes.

Two: Know Your Product Development Capability

To most executives, business fundamentals mean revenue, profit contribution, earnings per share, shareholder value, and other financially oriented data. While these criteria are important, they are the *results of* and not *contributions to* your operational wellness. Because these numbers are derived after the fact, they can only accurately reflect your corporate history—not your corporate future.

Relying on such sources of business intelligence is analogous to a general who attempts to win the war by reading a historian's account of it. Accountants and historians traditionally have much greater success at reporting what happened yesterday than predicting what will happen tomorrow. Accordingly, management's new role must be to operationalize initiatives that *create* the desired numbers rather than merely *react* to them.

Taking such initiatives is the only way to achieve long-term competitiveness. The reason is straightforward. The title of Most Competitive Company cannot be gained by mere financial manipulation. Competitiveness is *awarded* to you by your customers. It is *their perceived value of your products or services that either makes or breaks your business*. Therefore, one of your business objectives must be the creation of a product development capability that enables you to understand and satisfy the greatest number of customers.

Q. Where does your quest for competitive product development begin?

A. Understanding the need to address product development is one issue. Knowing where to begin is quite another. Chapter Four, Discerning the Past: The Source of Today's Problems, continues to build on the new insights presented in Chapters Two and Three.

Chapter Four examines in detail how decades of subconscious programming have influenced Western business's competitive ability, particularly in the areas of product cost, quality, timing, and reliability. An obvious conclusion is reached: Continued success requires a fresh approach to new product development. Chapter Five, The Results of Reality: A New Paradigm Emerges, explores and contrasts today's strategic business and product development thought with business realities. The current paradigm is challenged by relevant studies and case examples. In return, you are offered a simple, insightful, and competitive product development methodology for the 1990s.

Q. How difficult will it be to operationalize the new product development paradigm?

A. We've all heard the statement "Do it right the first time." However, you can't do something right the first time unless you know what the *it* is—the *it* being the product or service your customers want or need. Chapter Six, Operationalizing the New Paradigm, amplifies this concept. It explores why competitive product development must begin at the "customer/business" interface. It defines the principles you must apply. It also identifies the relationship and the benefits of achieving "right-first-time development" and "right-first-time operations" performance.

Q. How can my product development cycle be compressed?

A. Time is a constant. It cannot be compressed. Consequently, reducing your product development cycle means reengineering your current product development management processes. Achieving this objective requires control of the most frequently overlooked cycle reduction opportunity: earlier and more controlled product definition. Chapter Seven, Assuring Process Stability, explores why greater product definition control can significantly enhance the stability and effectiveness of your entire product development process.

Q. What is the most immediate product development cost reduction opportunity?

A. New product development generates change. However, there is no longer a need to continue forfeiting hundreds of thousands, if not millions, of profit dollars in processing *needless* product change. Chapter Eight, Effectively Managing Product Change, reveals how to reduce unnecessary change. More important, it discloses why expediting and controlling *necessary* change can save millions of dollars in unnecessary costs, increase your predictability of introducing new products on schedule, significantly improve customer satisfaction levels, and convert the process of change into a strategic advantage.

Q. How can the integrity of my products be improved?

A. For decades, businesses and customers have debated the question "Does the product you sold equal the product I bought?" Most manufacturers are unable to accurately answer this question during a product's development. Instead, they must wait until the end of the product development cycle to learn the answer. Not only is this process costly, but it debilitates customer satisfaction as well. Chapter Nine, Product

Integrity and Customer Satisfaction, discusses ways to avoid cost overruns and schedule delays that jeopardize product development, erode customer satisfaction, and needlessly tarnish your hard-earned corporate reputation. Chapter Nine also discusses how an increasingly important international standard (ISO 9000) adds another compelling reason why product integrity is such a critical factor for competitive success.

Three: Act Precisely and Decisively

Abe Lincoln was once quoted as saying, "If I had eight hours to fell a tree, I'd spend four hours sharpening my axe." His logic implies two key requirements: the need to *prepare* and the need to *act*. Too often, however, we just start "chopping" at problems without really understanding the underlying issues. For instance, when costs get out of line we start chopping (more appropriately called "right-sizing") to meet cost objectives. When new products are late to launch, we throw resources into the breach to "fix" the problem.

Because of their "ready-fire-aim" philosophy, few companies have really succeeded in operationalizing executive information systems, participative management, MRPII, total quality, project management, simultaneous engineering, or computer-aided anything. As a result, these initiatives exacerbate rather than resolve the real problems. Why can't we do it right?

There are several factors to consider. First, most executives admittedly are unable to visualize these strategic initiatives in sufficient detail to operationalize them effectively. Second, they are often unfamiliar with ways to launch the magnitude of organizational change these new initiatives require.

Chapter Ten, Energizing Your Organization for Action, provides a guide for action. While Chapters One through Nine discuss ways to analyse your performance and identify changes that must be made, Chapter Ten offers practical ways to make these changes happen. It defines the change process and offers a structured approach to carry through the major organizational changes needed to achieve the new product development paradigm.

CARPE DIEM (SEIZE THE DAY)

The military uses the phrase *decisively engaged* to describe opposing forces that can no longer maneuver and are fully committed to decisive battle. At this point, neither force can withdraw without suffering heavy casualties. Likewise, businesses around the world are decisively engaged in a war for competitiveness. The objective is to win the "hearts and minds" of the consumer. As you read these words, corporate battles are being fought to reduce costs, improve quality, and shorten the time required to develop new products. For the victors, the 1990s and beyond can be the most challenging decades in history.

For others, the call to arms will be the sound of collapsing markets and closing factories. Technological innovation, sophisticated customer demand, and worldwide competition are escalating at a relentless and unparalleled rate. Those who can successfully attack these issues will enjoy success. Those who fail may cease to exist.

Recall the three tenets modified from Sun Tzu's teachings: Know your competitors, know your customers, and know yourself; in a hundred trials you will never be in peril. While recent attempts to defend businesses against foreign competition have not been very successful, *you must remember that wars are not won by defensive skills; they are won by a well-executed offensive strategy*. The difference between victor and vanquished is often measured by the quality of executive leadership.

The success of tomorrow's effective product development capability must be built on the foundations already in place. As the Roman poet Horace wrote 2,000 years ago, *carpe diem;* it is time to seize the day!

Chapter Two

Deprogramming Your Subconscious

A ugust 8, 1945: From the skies rained force and fire of incalculable proportions. Within seconds, the infrastructure of Japan was virtually destroyed. Today, Japan, a nation smaller than the state of California, a country with virtually no natural resources, is taking on the best businesses in the world, and winning! Unquestionably, there must be a lesson to be learned here, if we are willing to discern it. The key word is *discernment*. Too often, we see but don't *discern*. We see, but we fail to comprehend the obscure issues that enable the success of the obvious. To quote the poet William Wordsworth, "We half create what we half perceive."

Perhaps this is why companies have difficulty internalizing the cost-cutting, quality-enhancing, or time-compressing approaches pioneered by Japanese industry. For example, the successes of product quality have been evident for more than 20 years. Yet few Western companies have effectively operationalized this simple methodology.

THE SUBCONSCIOUS
MANAGEMENT INFLUENCE

A primary reason for our inability to discern is subconsciously rooted in how Western and Eastern cultures experience the world around themselves. Perhaps these differences are the results of teaching and learning that began 2,500 years ago in ancient Greece. Here, the physician Hippocrates proposed a theory that a physical body was a holistic entity. He stressed a functional relationship between the parts and the whole, which, working in harmony and balance, created an "inner strength" or well-being.

Hippocrates was opposed by a contemporary, Democritus, who believed that man, as well as the universe, is nothing more than a composition of minute particles (atoms). Democritus taught that by treating these individual atoms, a physical body could experience strength and well-being. These two opposing philosophies became known, respectively, as "vitalism" and "atomism."[16]

Eastern cultures have never abandoned the philosophy of vitalism, also called Chi (pronounced *chee*), whereas the West has continued to pursue the more "scientifically respectable" philosophy of atomism. Seemingly from their graves, the ancient principles and orientations of Hippocrates and Democritus continue to subconsciously influence the way we manage today's product development. Not so?

A cursory comparison of vitalism and atomism reveals underlying differences in Eastern and Western management styles and the resulting influences on respective management approaches:

Atomism	*Vitalism*
Position	Teamness
Power	Harmony
Conflict	Oneness

Western atomism focuses on one's organizational level or position as a vehicle for ascribing authority and prestige. We reward the individual. In contrast, proponents of vitalism seek oneness; it is the team that shares successful achievement. Hence, our Eastern competitors' greater utilization and effectiveness of participative management and teaming initiatives should come as no surprise.

Knowing the differences in underlying motivation makes it much easier for us to understand the origin of today's Eastern management methodologies. More important, it provides insight into why these practices have been so difficult for us to adopt. So armed, we can further discern how the fundamental differences of atomism and vitalism are manifested in the philosophies of power/harmony and conflict/oneness.

These not-so-subtle influences also emerge in our differing approaches to product development. As an example, "Western scientists and engineers tend to study how the world works by analyzing the parts of a phenomenon of interest that are small enough to be understood separately. They then attempt to integrate this detailed knowledge into a description of the whole."[17] In contrast, their Eastern counterparts first create a vision of the whole and then decompose the vision into smaller and smaller parts to allow greater study and understanding. Perhaps this explains the Western tendency to develop products from a "bottom-up" perspective and the Eastern tendency to develop products from a "top-down" philosophy.

The difference between the bottom-up and top-down approaches can best be illustrated by the following comparison. When a group of U.S. automotive engineers was asked about their roles as members of a new-car design team, they replied, "We're designing component parts." In essence, these engineers design the "bits" without seeing the "whole." By default, someone else designs the car. This scenario represents an atomistic product development point of view.

In contrast, their competitors "holistically articulate a vision or a feeling" through the medium of design. For example, when Honda engineers began to design the third-generation Accord in the early 1980s, they did not start with a sketch of a car. Five sets of key words captured what the product leader envisioned: *open-minded, friendly communication, tough spirit, stress-free,* and *love forever. Tough spirit* in a car, for example, meant maneuverability, power, and sure handling in extreme driving conditions, while *love forever* translated into long-term reliability and customer satisfaction. Throughout the course of the project, these phrases provided a kind of shorthand to help people make coherent design and hardware choices in the face of competing demands.[18] In this case, Honda's product development approach, consciously or subconsciously, reflected a holistic (vitalistic) approach.

VITALISM, ATOMISM, AND PRODUCT DEVELOPMENT

Basic product development approaches can be attributed to management's adherence to the principle of either atomism or vitalism. Therefore, understanding each principle is essential to discerning the success of its application. With this purpose in mind, let's examine some contemporary examples of how these opposing influences have contributed to differing product development approaches.

Notice how vitalism supports teaming, harmony, and balance—a holistic perspective. Also notice how atomistic methodologies have an underlying emphasis on power, conflict, or divisiveness.

Atomism	Vitalism
Sequential product design	Simultaneous engineering
Competitive bidding	Supplier partnering
Multiple suppliers	Single sourcing
Contingency inventories	Just-in-time
Functional organizations	Cross functional teams
Product inspections	Statistical process control
Market research modeling	Listening to "customer whispers"
Engineering design	Design for assembly
Hierarchical management	Participative management
Islands of automation	Computer-integrated manufacturing

Source: Reprinted from *Industrial Engineering*, March 1991. Copyright 1991 Institute of Industrial Engineers, 25 Technology Park, Norcross, GA 30092.

This comparison suggests that there is sufficient correlation between the theories of vitalism and atomism to justify further examination of their impact on Eastern and Western product development strategies. Let's use a comparative ranking of key U.S. and Japanese product development initiatives as an analytic vehicle. The sequence of development and implementation of these initiatives implies important differences in respective product development perspectives.

For example, Japanese manufacturers began to improve their product development after first assessing their customers' desire for higher-quality products. They met this need by mastering statistical process control and other quality techniques. In contrast, early U.S. product improvement initiatives relied heavily on computer-aided design, robotics, and factory automation as the means to reduce product labor costs.

	Priority of Implementation	
Stragetic Initiative	Japan	U.S.
Customer needs assessment	1	10
Statistical process control	2	4
Simultaneous engineering	3	7
Just-in-time	4	5
Customer satisfaction	5	8
Vendor partnering	6	6
Computer-aided design	7	1
Automation and robotics	8	2
Computer-integrated manufacturing	9	3
Total quality management	10	9

What are the results of these differing perspectives on each competitor's current product development? By using the number, frequency, and periodicity of design change as the means of comparison, a product development model can be constructed to view the effectiveness of each approach (see Figure 2–1).[19]

The obvious question is, What is the cause for the striking difference in the number and frequency of change experienced within each profile? A second question might be, Could the differences in implementation scenarios

FIGURE 2–1
U.S./Japanese Product Development Comparison Model

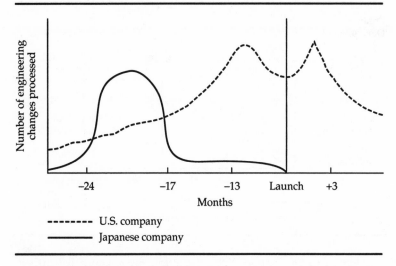

Source: Lawrence P. Sullivan, "Quality Function Development," *Quality Progress*, June 1986. Used with permission.

contribute to the variances exhibited by the model? Overlaying the implementation ranking on the model provides a unique insight into these questions.

THE JAPANESE APPROACH

The Japanese approach conforms to Japan's adoption of the principle of vitalism. Japanese manufacturers' holistic product development approach began with a thorough understanding of the wants of their customers. They then focused on the development and implementation of initiatives to satisfy those wants: high-quality, low-cost products and rapid response (see Figure 2–2). Notice in Figure 2–2 the balance between manufacturing and design initiatives—the attempt to achieve harmony and balance throughout the product development process.

FIGURE 2–2

Japanese Approach to Product Development Initiatives

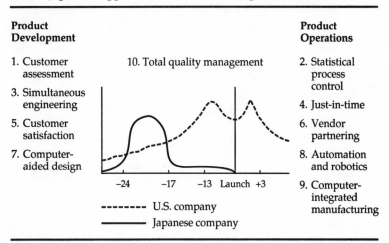

Product Development		Product Operations
1. Customer assessment	10. Total quality management	2. Statistical process control
3. Simultaneous engineering		4. Just-in-time
5. Customer satisfaction		6. Vendor partnering
7. Computer-aided design		8. Automation and robotics
	-24 -17 -13 Launch +3	9. Computer-integrated manufacturing
	- - - - - - U.S. company	
	———— Japanese company	

Also note in Figure 2–2 how each successive initiative "sets up" each succeeding methodology. For example, understanding the customer's desire (1) for quality and low cost initiated the statistical process control (SPC) initiative (2). The product consistency identified by SPC enabled simultaneous engineering (3) and just-in-time (4) to become a reality, and so on. By analyzing their priority of implementation, we see that *it is apparent the Japanese have focused more on holistically improving the effectiveness of their entire product development continuum than their U.S. competitors have.*

THE U.S. APPROACH

In contrast, U.S. manufacturers have followed a predictable subconscious atomistic philosophy (see Figure 2–3). This is evident by early emphasis on computerized design (1) and manufacturing automation (2, 3). However, despite investing billions of dollars in such technology-

FIGURE 2–3

U.S. Approach to Product Development Initiatives

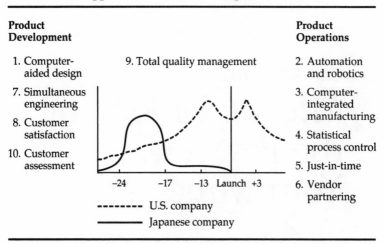

Product Development		Product Operations
1. Computer-aided design	9. Total quality management	2. Automation and robotics
7. Simultaneous engineering		3. Computer-integrated manufacturing
8. Customer satisfaction		4. Statistical process control
10. Customer assessment		5. Just-in-time
		6. Vendor partnering

-------- U.S. company
———— Japanese company

oriented initiatives, U.S. companies still find themselves enmeshed within islands of automation in lieu of computer-integrated manufacturing.

The success of this random product development strategy has been mixed at best. As a result, few companies are tackling the real initiatives required to achieve competitiveness: cycle compression, cost reduction, and improved product quality. Fewer still have been able to achieve an acceptable balance between satisfying customer wants, optimizing design engineering, and improving manufacturing productivity—the essence of competitive product development.

One issue has become clear. The degree of competitiveness between Eastern and Western manufacturers involves more than strategic intentions, bricks and mortar, management styles, or methodologies. The differences are much less obvious. They are to be discerned within the subconscious ways we have each been *programmed* to understand the nature of product development.

Chapter Three
Musubi: Unlocking the Power of Your Mind

A wareness of atomism and vitalism prepares one to see and internalize new principles and paradigms for success. Several of these principles are *balance, harmonious unification,* and *oneness.* Together they embody an uncomplicated yet powerful concept known as *musubi*—the practice of harmonious unification.[20]

Greater understanding of the principles of *musubi* can enable one to better develop the art of visualization, to see that which is invisible to others, and to visualize that which others can only intellectualize. The significance of being able to visualize your environment can be found in the following examples:

(1) A knowledgeable sports fan *sees* the game through the words of a radio commentator. He visualizes the quarterback scrambling to elude a blitzing defense, the game-winning double play, or the slow-motion magic of a three-point basket

at the buzzer. Another listener, who has no knowledge of the sport, is unable to relate to the same broadcast. The difference is not in the game. The difference is in the *knowledge* and *understanding* of what is to be visualized.

(2) In another case, a trained pilot "sees" his approach to a fog-enshrouded airport through the aircraft's instruments. The pilot's understanding of navigation, aircraft systems, and air-traffic control procedures enables him to immediately detect and correct out-of-balance conditions and complete a safe landing.

THE ART OF VISUALIZATION

Visualization requires an ability to identify key indicators and determine their patterns and tendencies on the whole. The greater your awareness and understanding of these indicators, the more lucid your visualization capability will be. As a point of illustration, take a moment to examine Figure 3–1.[21] At first glance, most observers see Pac-Man-type icons. Now stare at the bottom left grouping. Notice how a new relational pattern (a white triangular image) emerges once you've become attuned to visualizing it?

As this simple example illustrates, the power of visualization can enable you to see patterns and conceptual relationships where others may not. The most accurate instruments will not inform an untrained pilot whether he's on the right course or below the glide path. Nor can you achieve competitiveness without the ability to visualize, interpret, and integrate your key business readings.

Admittedly, visualization is not a simple task. The concepts of organizational balance, harmonious unification, and oneness are not taught in Western business schools.

FIGURE 3–1

The Art of Visualization

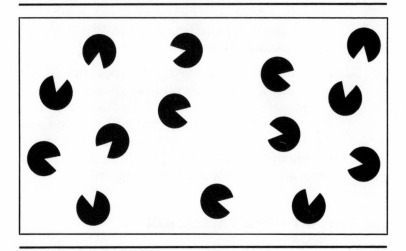

Source: Jearl Walker, "The Amateur Scientist," *Scientific American,* January 1988. Illustration by Hank Iken. Used with permission.

As a result, most executives are ill-prepared to implement them. Therefore, let's review these concepts within familiar experiences and scenarios.

BALANCE

Balance is a wonderfully fragile mechanism. A child's toy top, for example, achieves its balance when spun very quickly in a circular motion. On the lighter side, many employees feel their management attempts to maintain equilibrium in the same way—by going around in circles.

In contrast, balance within the human structure is maintained by a complex vestibular system. Minute changes in motion are continually monitored, detected, and interpreted. These impulses trigger constant subconscious corrective activity to maintain balance.

Unfortunately, maintaining balance in a product development environment is neither as simple nor as spontaneous as maintaining physical balance. The reason is that much of a product's development exists logically rather than physically. This makes the task of visualization more difficult. As a result, most "business vestibular systems" are not attuned to receive, interpret, or initiate the necessary corrective actions to balance their product development processes.

For example, in the early phase of new product development, a product is defined by requirements, specifications, drawings, and other types of data. During this stage of development, the product is typically "unseen" by management and is therefore beyond managers' conscious ability to receive or interpret. Data are inherently more difficult to assimilate and comprehend than a physical product is.

As development continues, these data are transformed into physical components, subassemblies, and finally a finished product. It is much easier to see and touch the problems encountered in a completed printed wiring assembly or a component than it is to identify problems in the data required to produce them. Similarly, most of the product's costs are also incurred before they become visible.

The combination of these criteria will typically cause you to look in the wrong direction for cost-reduction solutions. You can see excess and obsolete inventory, manufacturing cost overruns, and scheduling delays. However, without the ability to visualize a product's development, you won't be able to see the source of these problems.

As a result, *data development is the most difficult area in which to control costs. Regrettably, it is usually the primary source of product and process changes, expediting, rework, and overtime—issues that directly contribute to unplanned product development expenses.* Fortunately, as we shall discover, achieving a balanced product development process is more a matter of your approach than a matter of costly technology.

HARMONIOUS UNIFICATION

Harmonious unification is the result of successful and simultaneous integration of individual activities or processes to achieve a desired result. Now what does that statement really mean? I was struggling with how to illustrate the subtleties of this principle as my flight entered its final approach to Houston's Hobby Airport. During our taxi to the gate, I noticed a helicopter hovering near a taxiway intersection. Immediately, I knew I had serendipitously found the perfect example of harmonious unification: the act of hovering a helicopter.

Integrating versus Intellectualizing

In ground school, a student pilot studies the academics of flight: his aircraft's power plant, flight controls, and navigation and communication systems; physics; aerodynamics; and the environment in which the aircraft flies. While most student pilots can "intellectualize" these ground-school subjects, it is the visceral demands of flight that provide the greatest challenges. If it were not for having instructor pilots as their role models, most student pilots would be convinced that a helicopter is an impossible machine to fly.

The cause of this difficulty and doubt is that successful helicopter flight requires that the pilot achieve *musubi*— the ability to *balance* multiple inputs and outputs *simultaneously.* As anyone who has ever attempted to fly quickly realizes, learning the purpose of each flight control is relatively easy. The challenge is to correctly integrate them, or more appropriately, to experience harmonious unification. For example, bringing a helicopter to a hover requires the following:

(1) Adjusting the throttle with the left hand to maintain sufficient power to sustain flight.

(2) Using the left arm, raising or lowering the collective pitch lever to overcome weight and gravity causes the helicopter to rise and maintain a constant altitude above ground.

(3) Pressing the directional pedal with the appropriate foot to compensate for torque and control the helicopter's heading.

(4) Maintaining the helicopter's exact position and attitude by adjusting the cyclic control with the right arm.

(5) Visually maintaining safety clearance by constantly scanning for hazards and other aircraft with both eyes.

(6) Simultaneously monitoring the radio for air-traffic-control instructions.

Intellectually, it's all quite straightforward. However, *operationalizing* knowledge is quite another story. For example, if you wish to maintain hovering flight;

You must balance gravity and lift, which requires constant adjustment of collective pitch and engine power. A need for more lift decreases engine and rotor RPM, causing altitude to be lost. Increasing engine and rotor RPM generates more torque. More torque requires more antitorque pedal input to maintain directional control.

More antitorque pedal input requires more power,

decreasing engine and rotor RPM. Decreased engine and rotor RPM causes lift to be decreased, and altitude is lost. Lost altitude requires more throttle and collective pitch.

Whoops, a little too much collective pitch! Now you're hovering too high, so the whole process must be reversed. Meanwhile, you must constantly maintain attitude and position with the cyclic control stick, maintain safety clearance around the aircraft, and respond to air-traffic-control instructions.

Moreover, a successful hover requires that all these inputs and outputs occur simultaneously and in precisely correct amounts. *Only when the pilot has successfully mastered the integration of intellectual knowledge and proper corrective action can harmonious unification occur.*

Piloting Your Product Development Process

If we were to attempt to fly a helicopter like we've been trained to approach business problem solving, we would have already crashed! This is because we've been taught to address problems or issues atomically (one at a time). Like would-be jugglers, we're taught in business school, and by experience throughout our careers, how to juggle the red ball, then the blue, then the green one. While it may be true that we can juggle red, blue, and green balls, it is probably not safe to say that we can juggle them simultaneously. Therefore, is there any question why we have a budget meeting to discuss expenses, followed by a manufacturing meeting to review shipments, followed by a project design meeting to evaluate a new product's development, followed by a marketing meeting to analyze sales projections? Rather than becoming polished integrators, we have become very good at juggling one "business ball" at a time.

In contrast, a successful pilot envisions himself and his aircraft holistically. He continuously cross-checks his engine operations, flight plan, altitude, heading, and air speed. All the while, the pilot scans the horizon or monitors air-traffic control for any oncoming hazards. Subconsciously, the pilot and his machine become one entity. The pilot has experienced musubi.

The same need holds true for today's take-charge executive. Business stability requires an insightful business leader who can successfully *visualize* and *integrate* the processes and activities needed to operationalize a competitive product development methodology. The principle of harmonious unification recognizes that a product development process is an entity. It is not a collage of functional disciplines and activities that can be independently rearranged or changed at will. Like a skilled pilot, the executive also must venture beyond mere intellectual understanding to envision and integrate the individual product development activities and processes. This adds the power of action to the power of visualization—to interpret, integrate, and operationalize the information portrayed by the "business instruments."

ONENESS

The principle of holism, or oneness, is both an illusion and a competitive necessity. As such, oneness poses a dichotomy of values for most of us. For example, we aspire to emulate the results of successful teamwork from behind the walls we've built to protect our parochial "turfs." We think and act holistically by function, discipline, or department. It is a real stretch to even think, let alone act, as a holistic corporate entity.

However, the need for organizational oneness encompasses every functional element. It links us one to another. Oneness is an internalization of the corporate mission; it communicates a "larger-than-me" sense of purpose. Only when we see how we fit within the "corporate oneness" can we scale fiefdom walls and create an environment of mutual need and trust.

We can no longer suboptimize our industry, our company, our department, or ourselves and survive. The evidence of this fact all around us, for example:

- The outsourcing of management information systems (MIS) departments that choose to support technology rather than users.

- Engineers who design requirements without understanding manufacturing capabilities.

- Business managers who consume new product development resources on pet projects without concern for the impact on other business segments.

- Executives who trade seasoned "head count" for short-term margin contribution.

Yet as individuals and business leaders, we are bound by the limits of our humanity and our experience. We know what we know, are what we are, and do what we do because of what we've been taught. Within each of us, the subconscious patterns of Eastern or Western motivation have seeded different modalities to address the complexities of business and of product development in the 20th century.

Each of us is heavily influenced by the teachings of atomism or vitalism, by the principles of *musubi*, by balance or focus, by harmonious unification or one-at-a-time solutions, by oneness or individualism. The comparative results of these philosophies clearly show the need for dramatic change in the way we approach the design and, most important, how we manage the development of our new products. Future success demands that we break the chain of traditional management "think" and practice. If we are to regain the competitive advantage, we must purposefully challenge the ways of the past and the present.

Chapter Four

Discerning the Past: The Source of Today's Problems

S ince the industrial revolution, management has targeted the processes of manufacturing and assembly as the means by which to extract greater business performance. This trend continued throughout the 1980s, when manufacturers invested heavily in robotics and computer-aided design and manufacturing initiatives. Now, as we enter the 90s, several additional themes are attracting management's attention. One is, obviously, "the quality revolution." Another is reengineering, as companies struggle to survive the ravages of recession, competition, and the heavy debt loads of past mergers and acquisitions. There is also a potpourri of programs such as simultaneous engineering, design for assembly, electronic data interchange, flexible manufacturing, just-in-time, executive information systems, and other methodologies that

FIGURE 4–1

The Nature of Work

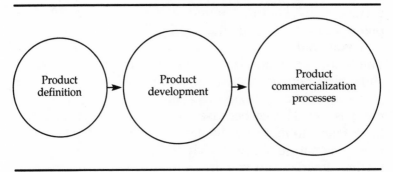

Source: Reprinted from *Industrial Engineering*, March 1991. Copyright 1991 Institute of Industrial Engineers, 25 Technology Park, Norcross, GA 30092.

consume much of management's valuable attention and resources.

How well have we capitalized on these themes? Are they contributing to the dramatic turnaround needed to get manufacturing businesses back on a competitive track? The answers are all around us. The automotive, electronics, and consumer products markets continue to erode. Corporate profits are down. Many of America's great wealth-creating enterprises such as Chrysler, General Motors, and IBM are fighting for their economic lives.

This is not the picture of competitive wellness. The question is, Why? Could it be that we have erred in our corporate courtship of these costly "theme solutions"? Or could it be that competitive wellness escapes us because we have been unable to correctly visualize how our businesses really work? (See Figure 4–1.)

THE NATURE OF WORK

"Nature-of-work" advocates have long espoused the theory "Where there are lots of people and lots of costs, there also must be lots of performance improvement opportunities." This usually translates into a strategy of fixing the processes involved in commercializing a product. A simpler definition is "fix manufacturing."

If you find yourself in this camp, you are not alone. The theory is emotionally appealing and may offer some short-term benefits. However, it is merely a continuation of an atomistic approach to a holistic product development issue. This is because nature-of-work proponents have failed to *discern* a diametrically opposed phenomenon—the nature of productivity influence. In essence, the further downstream you are in the development process, the less influence you have on your functional performance. For example, if you are in production, your efficiency is highly dependent on the accuracy of engineering designs, the timeliness of material support, and the accuracy and stability of marketing forecasts.

Conversely, little attention has been directed toward managing the productivity influencers at the *front end* of the business. As a result, management has misinterpreted the true nature of work for decades, namely, How do you define the products you wish to build?

As Figure 4–2 shows, nature-of-work promoters have failed to discern that the efficiency of a product's development is directly influenced by the adequacy and integrity of its definition, or more specifically, *what* it *is you're going to make.* This argument is further substantiated by the product development expenditure patterns of major industrial firms. Note how closely the mean resource expenditures for pre-product development, product development, and commercialization compare to the nature-of-work model.[22] (See Figure 4–3.)

In contrast, researchers have found that when companies increased their predevelopment emphasis, they correspondingly *increased the predictability of successful new product commercialization by a 2:1 ratio!*[23] Note again how this

FIGURE 4–2

The Nature of Productivity Influence

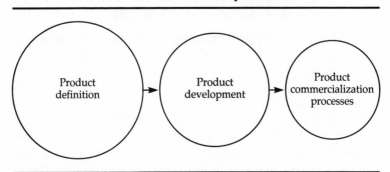

Source: Reprinted from *Industrial Engineering*, March 1991. Copyright 1991 Institute of Industrial Engineers, 25 Technology Park, Norcross, GA 30092.

finding substantiates the nature-of-productivity-influence theory. A comparison of successes to failures illustrates how these critical front-end steps can separate winners from losers:

- Winners spent more than twice as many resources on predevelopment activities than losers did.

FIGURE 4–3

Mean Expenditures for Primary Product Development Phases

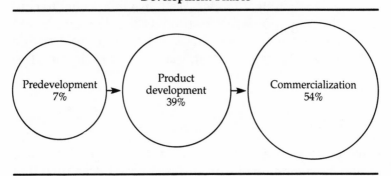

- Seventy-one percent of new product development was delayed due to poor definition and understanding of customer requirements.

- Changing product requirements induced more delays in product development than any other cause.

"Product losers typically sailed through the front-end stages with relatively little time and money spent. Perhaps because little or no homework was done, these projects ran into serious problems following their development stage. At this point, fixing commercialization problems required a disproportionate resource investment to turn the project around."[24]

PRAGMATISM AND PARADIGMS

Earlier, we contrasted the abilities of U.S. and Japanese manufacturers to define and control their product development processes. While only U.S. and Japanese approaches were depicted in this comparative model, similar conformity to the U.S. performance has been verified within the European Community as well. As a result, we've taken the liberty of changing the title to the Japanese/ Western comparative model. We'll use this model to contrast differing approaches to product development and to shed light on why most companies are finding it such a difficult task to improve cost, quality, and cycle compression objectives.

Timing of Product Definition

Change activity can be used as a measure to determine when the definition of a product has actually matured. For

FIGURE 4–4

Timing of Product Definition Achievement

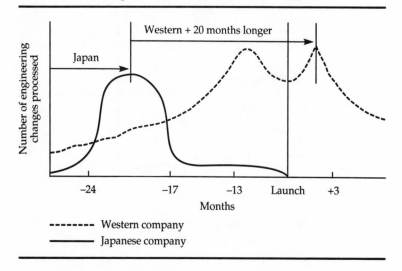

example, the lower the degree of change, the greater the maturity and the more a product is considered to be defined. Conversely, the higher the degree of change, the less a product is defined. Using this logic, Figure 4–4 shows that Japanese manufacturers define their products much earlier than Western manufacturers do.

In contrast to the Japanese model, the Western model represents a "we'll-know-it-when-we-see-it" product development philosophy. Unfortunately, this viewpoint is still ingrained in many manufacturing companies. The following account shows how a famous carmaker has personified this belief.

In this company, the development of a particular car emanated from a list of vehicle "features." This list of features was the source used to specify the car's "systems." Finally, detailed parts and components were derived and designed to achieve the systems' requirements. The features list defined the ambience of the car. It was the sun

FIGURE 4–5

"We'll-Know-It-When-We-See-It" Case Example

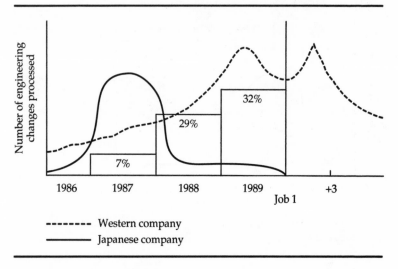

around which all developmental effort revolved. Because
of its strategic importance, the features list was held under
direct control of the executive leadership of the company.
It was also a very volatile document as well. For example,
in 1986, the executive team approved nearly 600 features
for the 1990 model car. Perhaps the executives were too
optimistic, because the closer they came to building the
car (Job 1), the more changes they made to the list (see
Figure 4–5).

In 1986 and 1987, 7 percent of the features were dropped.
The pace of change accelerated in 1988 when 29 percent of
the features were deleted before finally spurting to 32 percent immediately before Job 1. Note the correlation of
change to the Japanese/Western comparative model.

However, these changes only masked the real problem, which was that the features list defined the car systems, which in turn defined all of the detailed parts

design. One can only imagine answers to the following questions:

- What effect did the deletion of these features have on the car's perceived value and marketability?
- What effect did the addition and deletion of the vehicle's features have on the stability and effectiveness of the car's overall development processes?
- What effect did the addition and deletion of the vehicle's features have on the car's per unit costs?

The carmaker's "design-it-as-we-go" scenario corroborates the findings of the Japanese/Western comparative model. Unfortunately, this example is not unusual. It is the norm in scores of international companies. If you analyze your company's product definition philosophy, you may find a similar scenario. Regardless, you must discern whether you really do know your product needs or whether you will only know them when you've seen them.

Plateaus of Stability

A significant advantage of early product definition and control is the creation of a "plateau of stability" (see Figure 4–6). This plateau provides a high degree of stability to manufacturing operations, material procurement, and vendor partnering. The beneficial effects of stability on these downstream activities can be extraordinary.

Such was the experience of an aerospace/defense contractor. The contractor's product, a high-tech communication system, was continually beset by *operational problems*. For example, a study found that over 50 percent

FIGURE 4–6

Creating Plateaus of Stability

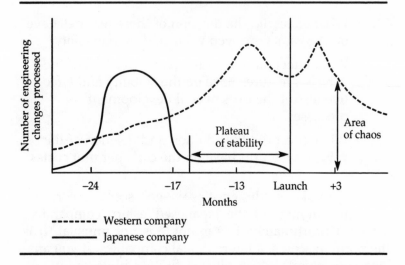

of the material kitted for release to manufacturing was unplanned. To make matters worse, nearly 75 percent of all planning packages issued to production were also unplanned.

The amount of *operational turbulence* generated by this magnitude of change caused excess material inventory, unnecessary overhead planning and administration costs, lower operational productivity, continuous schedule slippages, and unexpected cost overruns. In essence, manufacturing was in chaos.

These seemingly "operationally oriented" problems tend to reinforce the penchant of most businesses to embrace the nature-of-work theory. This is because operational problems generally have long incubation periods. Their symptoms often surface months after their original cause. This phenomenon can more accurately be shown by overlaying and comparing the aerospace/defense contrac-

FIGURE 4–7

Case Example: Product Development
Management Dynamics

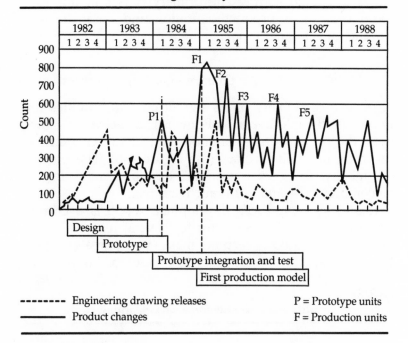

	1982	1983	1984	1985	1986	1987	1988
	1 2 3 4	1 2 3 4	1 2 3 4	1 2 3 4	1 2 3 4	1 2 3 4	1 2 3 4

Design
Prototype
Prototype integration and test
First production model

-------- Engineering drawing releases   P = Prototype units
———— Product changes   F = Production units

tor's product development schedule on the rate of change (see Figure 4–7).

Comparing change activity with the phases of a product's development is key to answering the obvious question, What caused the change "spikes" to occur? The first spike (P1) was caused by systems incompatibility problems discovered during prototype integration. The subsequent onslaught of changes required to fix the problem destabilized the entire material support and production processes. The resulting dynamics thwarted management's ability to control the product's remaining development prior to factory introduction. This caused the second spike to occur during the first production build (F1) and at each successive build. These spikes caused the operational chaos discussed above. The primary causes of this scenario were poor product definition and an ineffective product development management methodology.

Stability and Cycle Compression Opportunities

A plateau of stability offers significant opportunities for improving the effectiveness of downstream activities. However, the plateau's most ominous consideration could be its "compressibility factor" (see Figure 4–8). The greater its stability, the more a product's development cycle can be compressed—and with much less risk.

Reducing a product's development cycle is a critical competitiveness success factor for several reasons. First, your ability to quickly respond makes you a greater threat to your competition. This requires competitors' new prod-

FIGURE 4–8

Stability and Cycle Compression Opportunities

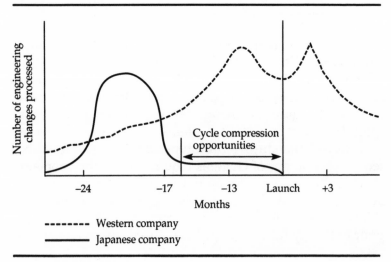

uct offerings to be "on target" and shortens their margin of opportunity. Conversely, this same advantage can work in your competitors' favor.

Second, you can more rapidly satisfy your customers' changing needs. This not only increases customer satisfaction but also raises the barrier to market entry and your competitiveness. Third, and perhaps more important, cycle compression accelerates a product's *time-to-volume* and *time-to-margin* contributions.

- *Time-to-volume* is the elapsed time required to achieve a product's optimum manufacturing rate.

- *Time-to-margin* is the elapsed time required to realize optimum margin contribution resulting from new product sales.

Obviously, the faster your manufacturing operations can ramp up to capacity, the faster you can reap a product's differentiated gross margin opportunities. Therefore, a primary purpose of compressing a product's development cycle is to *accelerate its time-to-margin* contribution (see Figure 4–9).

However, accelerating the time-to-volume ramp is extremely difficult, if not impossible, under the current Western new product development paradigm. This is because rework, design change, process change, and material shortages create a barrier between the optimal and typically achieved ramps. Removing or minimizing these obstacles is critical to competitive product development success. The following example of a computer manufacturer shows the cost of failing to manage these destabilizing factors.

At this manufacturer, product design changes were introduced late into the development cycle. This created numerous planning conflicts, material shortages, and pro-

FIGURE 4–9

Accelerated Time-to-Margin Contribution

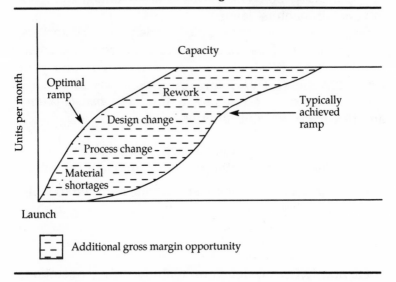

Additional gross margin opportunity

cess adjustments. The combined effect of these actions caused production to fall to nearly 70,000 units under plan. The shortfall represented a $55 million gross margin opportunity loss—on one product! Given the increasing rates of product obsolescence, difficulties in maintaining product differentiation, and shrinking profit margins, you must optimize your time-to-volume and time-to-margin opportunities. Failure to achieve these critical success factors can spell the difference between business competitiveness and business mediocrity.

Achieving Product Reliability, Maintainability, and Quality Targets

The Japanese/Western comparative model also reveals a significant barrier that has prevented Western management from achieving acceptable product reliability, main-

FIGURE 4–10
Achieving Product Reliability, Maintainability, and Quality Targets

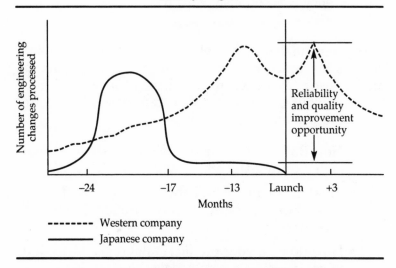

tainability, and quality targets (see Figure 4–10). *The closer our products get to manufacturing launch, the more changes we make!* Could this finding indicate a Western inability to define a product before it can really be seen?

At best, improving product reliability, maintainability, or quality performance is difficult within a stable product development environment. Earlier, we discussed the case of a carmaker who frequently changed its features list. The carmaker also painfully discovered that a high degree of change at product launch represented an insurmountable barrier to its quality and reliability objectives. The unmanaged product change caused

- Every vehicle at final build to be short nearly 20 component parts.

- Twenty-five percent of all final build workmanship problems.

- Such a degree of *informational turbulence* and *assimilation overload* that the overall operational efficiency was seriously impaired.

The potential quality, reliability, and maintainability impacts illustrated by the Japanese/Western comparative model pose a few questions that demand answers. For example, if your company fits this scenario and you introduce your products on schedule,

- How do you accommodate all of the changes generated during and after manufacturing?
- What is the difference between the first and last version of your most recently introduced new products?
- How do you, your product support channels, and your customers accommodate these product changes?

Containing Product Development Costs

Changes are direct contributors to unplanned product development costs. Assuming a scale of 0 to 300 product changes, Western companies generate three times more change activity than their Japanese competitors (see Figure 4–11). This equates to approximately $5.6 and $1.7 million in respective change administration costs alone!

The cost of change experienced by the Western companies we have discussed underscores their difficulty in reducing product costs. For example,

- The aerospace contractor's program changes exceeded $50 million. In retrospect, many of these costs were unnecessary.

FIGURE 4–11

Containing Product Development Costs

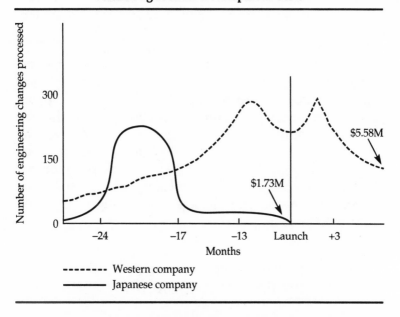

• The computer manufacturer's case was much more severe. Its annual costs of change exceeded $21 million. This equated to more than 420,000 hours of non-value-added work requirements. The company lost nearly $55 million in gross margin opportunity on one product. Failure to effectively manage its product development processes put the company's entire $1.5 billion international business at risk because of noncompliance to ISO 9000.

• The automaker's annual cost of change exceeded $41 million dollars.

Regrettably, these are not hypothetical numbers. They are examples that can be found in companies around the world, companies just like yours. More important, they reflect missed cost reduction and lost profit contribution opportunities that could have made these companies more competitive.

Unfortunately, the comparative model does not reflect an isolated theory. Instead, it is widely supported by additional empirical data. A recent study of international aerospace, defense, textiles, electronics, and consumer products manufacturers and construction, utility, ship repair, and foundry companies disclosed that these companies experienced an average of 330 design changes per month. (The range was 2 to 1,000 changes per month.) How do your company's statistics compare to these? More important, how do you manage your change activity or accommodate its impacts?

INSTITUTIONALIZED PRODUCT DEVELOPMENT INADEQUACIES

Given the toll in reduced productivity and lost profit contribution, it is difficult to understand why so many companies choose to "institutionalize" their product development inadequacies rather than tackling them head-on. This tendency is evident in the following examples:

- An automotive manufacturer typically *plans* nearly 200 design engineering man-years to "optimize" component designs, from the power train to the sun visor, after the vehicle has been fully prototyped.

- A high-tech office equipment manufacturer usually *plans* for five design iterations of a new product before the product is released into manufacturing.

- A defense manufacturer traditionally *plans* for a 300 percent rate of design change.

- An aircraft manufacturer habitually *inflates* its fabrication lead times by 50 percent to allow for anticipated and uncontrolled design changes.

The inclination to institutionalize these wasteful practices was evident in Figure 2–1, in which the wide differences in allocation of time between development and manufacturing is apparent. Given the discussions in this chapter, are these widely divergent capabilities a reflection of an ability or inability to

- Understand customer needs and wants?

- Define and control a product's development?

- Compress the development cycle?

- Optimize manufacturing to achieve time-to-volume and time-to-margin opportunities?

In any event, institutionalized product development inadequacies are not a promising foundation for U.S. competitiveness. It is much more difficult to be a product leader if it takes you twice as long as your competitors to convert an idea into a new product. Your crystal ball must have twice the range and clarity.

Xerox experienced this painful lesson in the 1980s. In the mid-1970s, Xerox controlled 95 percent of the worldwide copier market. By 1983, its share had nose-dived to 50 percent—in no small part because Japanese product development cycles were less than half of Xerox's.[25]

Nor does the product development scenario discussed in this chapter provide the rapid response time necessary to enable the United States to be a viable follower. The result of continuing these practices is a "lose-lose" scenario. Fortunately, purposeful and knowledgeable business leaders can turn such a noncompetitive situation around.

Chapter Five

The Results of Reality: A New Paradigm Emerges

For decades, Western businesses have followed a philosophical course that seeks answers to two key questions: (1) What are we good at? and (2) How can we use this expertise to make products that will optimize our assets? This rationale is still the foundation of much of our current "business think," and it is inherent within the latest strategic business theories from core competency, to product differentiation, to benchmarking. Unfortunately, this is only renaming an outmoded theory—What's good for Detroit is good for the people. In essence, these current theories perpetuate the old philosophy of "Build a better mousetrap and the world will beat a path to your door."

As today's paradigm suggests, this outlook still causes many businesses to project *from* their business *to* their markets (see Figure 5–1). Businesses create new products, take new initiatives, reengineer new organizational struc-

FIGURE 5–1

Today's Product Development Paradigm

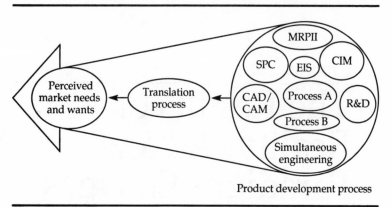

Product development process

tures, and develop new processes that are good—from the company's point of view. They then translate these core competencies and asset bases into product and service "offerings" to be made *available* for the *perceived market*.

The world's most innovative companies are particularly susceptible to this phenomenon. For example, Apple Computer's chairman, John Sculley, blames a lot of the problems that caused a three-year slip in market share on corporate myopia. Sculley stated, "We've been looking inward too much."[26] Another premier product development company found the need to woo back sticker-shocked customers. Michael J. Jackson, of Mercedes Benz's U.S. marketing office, concedes that "until now, the company had marketed its cars with little regard for the changing marketplace."[27]

A recent international business survey suggests reasons why companies follow this inwardly focused approach. Findings reveal that as late as 1989, "47 percent of today's companies were still unclear about their customers' needs!"[28] Furthermore, their processes for identifying new product opportunities were based on the following criteria:

Basis of Assessment	Percentage
Discussion/consensus	47
"Gut feel"	23
Return on investment	13
Risks versus costs	8
Profit potential	6
Other	3

Source: Reprinted with permission from David M. Reid, "Where Planning Fails in Practice," *Long Range Planning*, vol. 23, no. 2 (1990), pp. 85–93.

Twenty-three percent reliance on "gut feel"? Gut feel does not reflect an understanding of the needs and wants of potential customers. Gut feel cannot form the basis of competitive product development. Unfortunately, these inwardly focused methods still represent the product development paradigm embraced by too many of today's businesses.

In view of the escalating "emphasis-on-the-customer" initiatives espoused by many businesses, it is difficult to believe this perspective continues to exist. However, the mean expenditures for market research and assessment corroborates the survey's findings. Respondents spent nearly four times as much to validate *what they had made* as they spent to decide *what they should be making*.[29]

A TIME FOR ACTION

The facts are unmistakable. Western businesses continue to inadequately address their product development problems. They have not focused on the right issues or targets. Nor have they realized that the path to competitiveness must begin with a thorough understanding of the customers and their preferences.

To the contrary, evidence strongly suggests that today's product development strategies are still based on the theories of protectionism, asset management, core competence, and differentiation—and, too often, corporate arrogance. The common denominator of these strategies is as follows:

- Development and protection of internal proprietary technologies—whether or not they add competitive product value.

- Creation of "best-in-class" product development processes—whether or not they add perceived customer value.

- Conversion of technologies and capabilities to make products and services available to the market—whether or not they are needed or wanted.

- Continuance of corporate "we-know-best" arrogance—whether or not corporations understand their customers' wants or needs.

The unspoken thesis of this strategy is, Protect your technologies and assets by making products available for customers. This is a survivalist mousetrap-maker's philosophy—not a competitor's! If we take away one lesson from this chapter, it should be that today's unrelenting competition has taught two painful truths:

(1) You cannot continue to make available what you can to utilize the assets you've got.

(2) If you always do what you've always done, you'll always get what you've always gotten.

Instead, you must develop a new, strategic "customer-to-business" new product development orientation.

Unfortunately, old ways die hard. Past strategies are difficult to change. They become inculcated in our processes, procedures, subconscious business practices, organizational structures, and corporate cultures. A Latin phrase epitomizes this phenomenon: *Abeunt studia in mores* (Practices zealously pursued pass into habits). To be successful, you must discern outdated habits and practices, and replace them with more competitive ones.

A NEW PARADIGM EMERGES

The findings discussed previously of the nature-of-productivity model, the business study, and the Japanese/Western comparative model are clear: *Unless a product is adequately defined and controlled early in its development, communicative and interpretative dynamics will be introduced into each succeeding product development process.* If left uncontrolled, these dynamics can destroy the integrity of your products. More important, they can destabilize the people and the processes required to create them.

A key principle of effective product development emerges from these findings: *The further downstream a product is defined in its development process, the less control individual elements have on their productivity, and the more effort, time, and cost are incurred.* Conversely, *the further upstream a product is defined in its development process, the more control individual elements can exert upon their productivity, and the less effort, time, and cost are incurred.*

Consequently, tomorrow's competitive businesses will be those that can do the following:

- Embrace a basic truth. The only reason for a
  profit-making business to exist is to create prod-

FIGURE 5–2
The Competitive Product Development Paradigm

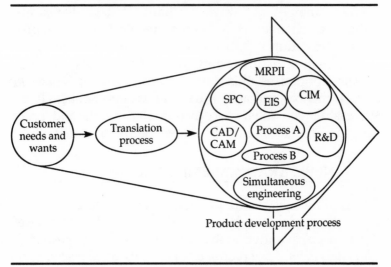

Product development process

ucts or services that satisfy the wants or needs of customers.

• Stop addressing the atomic bits of their business and holistically address the purpose of their business—the effective development of innovative new products that meet customer expectations.

• Refuse to forfeit their business to competitors who can better identify and satisfy customer requirements.

Accomplishing these objectives means being able to visualize and operationalize a new product development paradigm, one that has a reengineered focus extending *from* the customer/business interface *to* the business (see Figure 5–2).

If businesses are to realize this new paradigm, they must adopt an immediate three-step process:

Step 1. Identify, understand, and quantify the needs and wants of your potential customers.

Step 2. Rationalize your existing products against these customer expectations.

Step 3. Tailor your people, processes, and information requirements to efficiently translate customer needs and wants into products that meet these expectations.

Many businesses may find that these three steps characterize a major departure, a paradigm shift from their current product development approach. However, as we've just reviewed, nothing less than a paradigm shift will enable them to survive as major competitors. For most, the question is not whether they need to change but rather how and where to begin the transition to a more competitive product development process. If by now you believe competitiveness is awarded to you by your customers, then you must begin your competitiveness quest where potential customers meet your business. This point is called the *customer/business interface*.

The Customer/Business Interface

What is the customer/business interface? The customer/business interface is not merely a reference point. It is a physical event where you and your customer have an opportunity to view each other—and where each party makes a critical decision. These decisions are, Which product should I buy? and Which product should I make?

In essence, the customer/business interface is a two-way mirror. From one direction, it reflects your product's value as perceived by the customer. From the other, it enables you to discern specific product wants and needs that cause potential customers to decide to buy.

The customer/business interface is where potential customers "evaluate" the attributes of your products. It is their perceived value of these attributes, not yours, that will cause them to buy or reject your product, to cast their vote for or against your competitiveness. Therefore, it is important to understand the relationship of your product attributes and their perceived customer value.

Product Attributes

A product *attribute* is an inherent characteristic or feature that can be measured or evaluated. As discussed in Chapter Two, for Honda's third-generation Accord, these attributes were captured in five sets of key words: *open-minded, friendly communication, tough spirit, stress-free,* and *love forever*. Individually and as a whole, these key words reinforced the car's message to consumers. *Tough spirit,* for example, meant maneuverability, power, and sure handling in extreme driving conditions, while *love forever* translated into long-term reliability and customer satisfaction.

While attributes provide an important evaluative starting point, they are not easily defined. For example, while cars can easily be ranked and compared by cost or horsepower, other attributes are not so absolutely measured. How does a customer value luxury or performance? To find the answer, you must define the *contributors* to each attribute. Some contributors to luxury might be the following:

- The vehicle's name (e.g., Cadillac or Rolls Royce).
- Quietness of operation.
- Automotive awards acclaim.
- Natural versus synthetic materials.

- Quality of accessories.
- Comfortable appointments.

Perceived Customer Value

There are several reasons for defining your product attributes and their contributors. First, you can quantitatively learn their respective value as perceived by potential customers. In turn, these perceived customer values can enable you to determine the following:

- Which product features prospective customers want or need.

- What technologies, skills, and processes are required to convert these needs and wants into desirable products and services.

- The desirability of your product's features and the estimated value customers may be willing to pay for them.

- How to position your products against those of your competitors for maximum profit opportunities.

To be of merit, these perceived attributes and their contributors must be heuristically or quantitatively determined and evaluated (see Figure 5–3). For example, what is the perceived value of the acclaim of automotive awards on a customer's buying decision? More important, what would the customer most likely be willing to pay if such acclaim and recognition could be achieved?

Second, the more you understand a product's attribute and contributor *values*, the earlier and more accurately you can define your new products. Let's see how this might have helped our international carmaker. Had the carmak-

FIGURE 5–3

Examples of Perceived Feature Values

Contributors	Measures of Perceived Value		
	Heuristic		Quantitative
Name (e.g., Cadillac or Rolls Royce)	+ + + +	High	$2,000
Quietness of operation	+ +	Med	$1,000
Automotive awards acclaim	+	Low	$500
Natural vs. synthetic materials	+ + +	High	$1,500
Quality accessories	+ +	Med	$1,200
Comfortable appointments	+ + +	High	$1,500

er's executives better understood their product's attribute and contributor values, they might have earlier and more accurately defined their features list. They also might have prevented the costs incurred from the continual change of these features.

Third, attributes and contributors have a direct impact on sales and development costs. For example, it doesn't matter

- How much you improve the quality of a product feature if it has minimal perceived customer value.

- How critical a core competency might appear to be if it doesn't add to the customer's perceived value.

- How much you improve a process's efficiency if it doesn't produce a product that customers value.

- How much you spend on a new advertising campaign if the product's attributes and contributors do not meet the customer's expectations.

Finally, increasing the perceived value of a product should have a direct correlation to an increase in its sales revenue. The more a product's attributes satisfy customers' needs or wants, the more favorable their buying decisions should be. Similarly, a product or a product feature that has little added value should be a candidate for elimination or cost reduction.

Our international carmaker used this methodology to trim product costs. The carmaker's analysis revealed expensive features, oversized oil filters, and other types of unique and costly components. An equally important finding was that many of these attributes were *transparent* to customers. As a result, they had minimal impact on customers' perceived attribute value. While these product features contributed to the cost of the product, they had no positive contribution to sales!

Many companies have yet to embrace this tenet of perceived attribute value of the new product development paradigm—even in the face of overwhelming success by their competitors. However, one country has mastered the concept. By listening to "the whispers" of customers, Japanese manufacturers have made significant inroads into the economy-to-luxury auto market. They have dominated the consumer electronics and the computer products industries. They have accomplished all of this by first capturing the desires of the customer. Second, they are able to rapidly convert customer desires into exciting quality products. Evidence abounds that they are winning the battle for competitiveness. Moreover, *they are winning the battle for competitiveness at the customer/business interface.*

Selling versus Making

Admittedly, achieving a paradigm shift will take time. However, recognizing the need to change is an important first step. As a senior auto executive recently stated, "We're just beginning to realize our mission is to *sell* cars—not just *make* them." What a radical strategic departure! *Making* represents the current product development paradigm. *Making* implies using technology and assets to make products available for customers. In contrast, *selling* implies understanding and satisfying customers. *Selling* implies converting customer needs and wants into new products—before the competition does. *Selling* implies the efficient integration of processes, people, and technology to reduce costs and improve product integrity. This is the foundation of the new product development paradigm, and the time to begin is now.

Why is this seemingly straightforward paradigm so difficult to put into practice? There are several rationalizations. First, the paradigm's basic principles may be the Business Integration 101 course your business school professors didn't teach you. Consequently, you don't perceive new product development as a strategic executive issue. Nor does it carry as much emotional excitement or promotional value as winning the Malcolm Baldrige award. Or perhaps new product development is just psychologically perceived as the "grubby" side of management that Drucker warned us about.

The second rationalization is that the new paradigm requires major changes in strategic and tactical business "think." In many respects, it may be a complete reversal of the beliefs on which typical product development has been based for centuries. This demands taking a risk to think "out of the box." Like other pathfinders, you may find that going against the grain of conventional thought demands much more than your personal understanding. It requires your personal leadership, your personal conviction, and your personal courage.

Chapter Six

Operationalizing the New Paradigm

C larity of a product's definition and stability of its development are critical success factors for improving operational competitiveness. By maintaining clarity of what it is that you expect to create, you facilitate mutual understanding and communication of what the *it* is. In turn, this provides greater stability of the many processes required to develop it.

Regrettably, this logical approach does not occur naturally. Operationalizing and sustaining a stable and predictable product development environment requires adoption of a revitalized product development management (PDM) methodology. PDM is not just another new version of the bureaucratic product development gauntlets of the past, but a truly revitalized approach. The PDM approach is not a cookbook, a daunting list of rules, or a burdensome set of procedures. Instead, PDM is a philosophy, a methodology, a discipline, a corporate mind-set. It is a corporate way of life that operationalizes the intent of quality champion W. E. Conway: "Do it right the first time."

Inherent within this worthy objective are two key variables: the *do* and the *it*. The *do* refers to the skills and the processes required to develop a product, whereas the *it* defines the product. *Do* has been the traditional focus of nature-of-work advocates. *Do* is the most visceral, visible, and seemingly important half of the new product development equation. Therefore, organizational structures and functions are created to do the *do*. Management of the *do* has been studied, processed, and proceduralized. Hundreds of books have been written about ways to execute the *do* better. Businesses even benchmark and measure how they're doing against world-class *do*.

On the other hand, the *it* is the Rodney Dangerfield of product development. *It* gets no respect. Few companies recognize that the *it* must precede the *do*. Fewer have structures or functions to define, communicate, or manage their *it(s)*. *It* is seldom the subject of a book or a study. Nor is *it* often considered, studied, benchmarked, or measured. As a result, most businesses have yet to discern the importance of the *it*. A scant number realize that *the role of an effective product development methodology is to harmoniously integrate the* do *and the* it. Fewer realize that this means the *it* must be understood and defined *before* it can be done right the first time. Equally important, definition of the *it* must be maintained if you expect to continue doing it right. For example,

- An engineer can design a magnificent solution to a complex requirement, only to find that the requirement has been changed.

- A machinist can produce a part of the strictest tolerance, only to discover that it is now the wrong part.

- A company can produce the finest product, only to discover that the product no longer meets customer expectations.

In each case, the *do* was properly accomplished. At the time the *do* was initiated, the *it* was also correct and accurate. So what went wrong? The error was in failing to integrate, communicate, and maintain a constant awareness of the relationship between the two.

The product development tasks were begun with one understanding of the *it*. Then, for some reason the definition changed. Success was now measured by a new and different definition. Is this an anomaly? The answer is a resounding no!

Properly defining and maintaining the definition of an *it* is a constant problem. Operationalizing a solution to how this can be done is the role of an effective product development management (PDM) methodology. In essence, PDM is the discipline by which your organization can understand, articulate, communicate, and control this elusive *it*.

PRODUCT DEVELOPMENT MANAGEMENT PRINCIPLES

Revitalized product development management is an innovative and straightforward approach. Four principles are involved: product definition, definition control, change control, and incorporation. Together they form a highly

integrated and disciplined methodology to facilitate the
operationalization of a new and more holistic product development
paradigm. The purposes of these principles are
as follows:

- *To define the product.* The desired product must be
  defined early in its development, with sufficient
  detail and clarity to enable others to understand
  and take action to achieve it. Product definition is
  the articulation of your strategic product development
  vision.

- *To control this definition.* Disciplines must be put in
  place to maintain the accurate translation of a
  product's definition into the many languages
  required to create it. Definition control is necessary
  to assure the integrity and stability of a product's
  development cycle. Product definition control
  is a methodology for operationalizing your strategic
  product vision.

- *To aggressively manage change.* A new product is
  typically defined iteratively. This means that its
  definition will most likely change during its life
  cycle. Therefore, a process must be introduced to
  ensure that all change to the product contributes
  to its integrity, stability, and intent. Product
  change control is a way to control your product
  vision.

- *To assure that change is made as planned.* Once
  changes have been approved, an effective incorporation
  process assures they are implemented as
  effectively and accurately as planned. Product
  change incorporation is your product integrity
  assurance.

Operationalizing these principles involves the interaction of three inseparable criteria: definition and communication of the *it*, the product development *process*, and the *organizational elements* that must translate this definition to create the product.

COMMUNICATING THE *IT*

Communicating a product's definition is inherently complex. There are several reasons for this. First, the definition must be early in the product development process, where most uncertainties exist. Second, the need for communication of a product's definition is widespread and takes many forms, such as product specifications, drawings, bills of material, test requirements, technical publications, business operating systems, process instructions, cost accounts, product introduction activities, sales and user training, human resource recruiting, and capital expenditures. Virtually every aspect and constituent of your business utilizes elements of a product's definition.

Third, it is difficult to control, communicate, and translate a product's definition. We probably can all remember the parlor game in which someone is given a whispered message. In turn, this person whispers the message to another, who whispers what he heard, and so the game goes. Finally, the last person in line recites his version of the message. Remember how everyone laughs when the original intent of the message is lost through translational errors? However, this scene is not as laughable when communication of a product's definition is lost during its development. Nor is it as humorous to the functional "doers," those in the trenches actually building your new products, when they are condemned to work in an unstable and "fuzzy" business environment.

The Fuzzy Company

Fuzzy companies are more prevalent than most people realize. They exist throughout the international business world. Fuzzy companies are the outgrowth of imprecise product communication, organizational fiefdoms, and bureaucratic development processes. You may be unknowingly leading or working in one right now. Go ahead. Take a hard look at your company. You probably won't see a fuzzy company. This is because a fuzzy company environment is usually imperceptible from an insider's point of view. There are several reasons for this.

First, a fuzzy company evolves because of the way we've been programmed to communicate with one another—anecdotally and without precision of context. We use terms like *premier, elite,* or *world-class* to describe our products, services, and even ourselves. These descriptors are akin to terms such as *furniture* or *groceries*. We only *think* we are communicating when we use them. This is because they are open for dissimilar interpretation of meaning and achievability. Just check the contents of shopping carts the next time you're waiting in the checkout line at your neighborhood grocery. While no two shoppers will purchase exactly the same items, each is buying his or her personal version of groceries.

Similarly, anecdotal product definition creates a fuzzy working environment, which in turn causes process and product instability. This instability is the source of redundant effort, avoidable change, unnecessary rework, and functional incompatibilities. Unless these factors are addressed and corrected, functional elements will compensate for them by *institutionalizing* coping measures. These measures typically include stretching schedules, padding budget estimates, and banking resource requirements—all of which will incrementally inflate your product devel-

opment costs. In some companies, this subconscious inflation has exceeded 50 percent!

*The second reason for continuance of a fuzzy business environ-
ment is that it provides a safe haven.* Management doesn't
have to set tough strategic product development objectives. Marketing doesn't have to "belly up" to the responsibility of defining new products to satisfy customer
wants. Engineering can point at manufacturing problems
and say, "That's not the way we designed that widget."
Manufacturing is free to interpret engineering documentation. Vendors can ship what they think you ordered. In
essence, a fuzzy business environment precludes something management avoids most—real accountability.

Third, a fuzzy company evolves slowly over time. As a result,
non-value-added coping mechanisms become ingrained.
Many companies have raised the concept of *Abeunt studia
in mores* to an art form! We've already been exposed to
several of them:

- The automotive manufacturer that *planned* nearly
  300 design engineering man-years to "optimize"
  component designs after prototype. At $100,000
  per engineer, this represents a $30 million annual
  engineering savings opportunity—per new car
  program!

- The high-tech office equipment manufacturer that
  planned for five design iterations. How can a
  "right-fifth-time" company compete against a
  "right-first-time" competitor?

- The defense manufacturer that traditionally
  planned for a 300 percent rate of design change.
  Can a company accept this degree of operational
  chaos and added product cost, and still be
  competitive?

- The aircraft manufacturer that habitually *inflated* fabrication lead times by 50 percent to allow for anticipated and uncontrolled design changes.
  How does this history of inflation impact the company's cycle compression and product cost reduction initiatives?

PRODUCT DEVELOPMENT: THE PROCESS

Managing product development is not a revolutionary new concept. Most companies have adopted some form of new product development process. The automotive sector has "concept-to-customer" and "four-phase" approaches. Others have developed their own versions. Regardless of their intent, traditional product development approaches generally fall within two categories. The first is a formalized, stringent, and uncompromising technical process that stifles organizational flexibility and creativity. The second is so undefined that it only adds another program to the list of "nonimplemented shelfware." Neither approach fits today's competitive scenario.

An uncompromising technical process acts as a barrier to be bypassed by functional "doers." As one chief engineer stated, "The value of experience is knowing how to get around the process." In contrast, an unimplemented process serves no value, except to provide a security blanket for management.

As a result, these product development approaches are more hype than reality. Most hinder more than they help. Few fulfill their intended purpose—to facilitate and channel an organization's creativity toward satisfying customer needs. The importance of this issue cannot be overstated. For every day you perpetuate an ineffective product development process, the less competitive you become.

Customers are becoming increasingly more, not less, knowledgeable and sophisticated. In turn, they are de-

FIGURE 6–1

New Product Development: A Structured Process

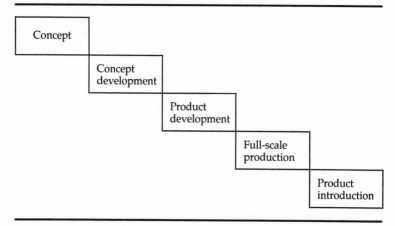

manding a greater, not lesser, array of innovative and complex products. Who will meet these challenges?

The answer is, the most talented, creative, and innovative people. Therefore, an effective product development process must balance and integrate creative people needs with those of effective supporting processes. This requires a structure to nourish and channel creativity, and a responsive decision process to manage it.

Structure

The purpose of a structure is to provide a framework for identifying the critical new product development activities and the phases in which they must occur. Creating the structure is a fundamental step. It provides the timing and the means for identifying, defining, communicating, translating, and controlling the tasks necessary to transform a product's definition into its finished configuration (see Figure 6–1).

While accomplishing this critical step might appear to

FIGURE 6–2
   New Product Development: Opposing Perspectives

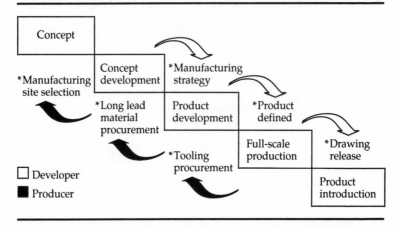

be simple, it is not. This is because its success requires businesswide, cross-functional input and reconciliation of two diverse perspectives. These perspectives represent the opposing needs of a product's developers and its producers (see Figure 6–2).

A Developer's Perspective

The development of a product is generally planned *from left to right*, from today into the future. There are two primary reasons for this. The first is obvious: You can only work in the present and the future, not in the past. The second reason is less apparent and more difficult to overcome, because it is founded in fear: fear of the unknown, fear of making a costly mistake, fear of being wrong. A primary source of this fear is an inadequate understanding of customer's needs. In this mode, developers schedule key decisions and activities as late into development as possible. They are primarily motivated to (1) provide time to define the product and (2) reduce the risks of unknown variables that should have been resolved early in the product's definition.

These practices are so predictable that they could be considered a law of product development: *The more a company's culture is risk averse, the further product development decisions will be delayed to the right.* This law is often typified, for example, by marketing's reluctance to adequately define a product until the prototype has successfully passed several customer evaluations, or by engineering's failure to release their drawings until the design is required to be transferred to manufacturing. In either case, the developer's perceived fear of being wrong holds a greater penalty than the reward of being right.

A Producer's Perspective

Typically, the production of a product is usually planned *from right to left*, from the introduction date backward. A producer's primary objective is to reduce the risks of unknown variables that may occur early during a product's production. This practice is so foreseen that it could be considered an opposing law of product development: *The more a company's culture is risk averse, the further product production decisions will be accelerated to the left.* This is often typified by the example of manufacturing's arguments for long-lead material or tooling decisions early in a product's development.

A properly defined product development structure will enable a manufacturer to recognize these divergent product development perspectives. More important, it provides the means to satisfactorily negotiate and integrate when and where these key activities should occur. A comprehensive product development structure is a prerequisite for balancing and managing these diverse product development perspectives.

FIGURE 6–3
Channeling New Product Development Creativity

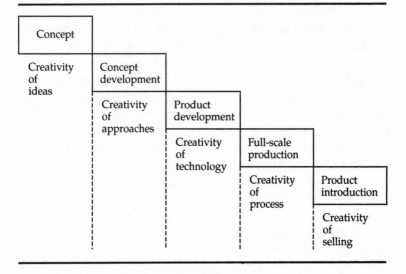

Channeling Creativity

Creativity is essential for accelerating the development of innovative, low-cost, high-quality new products. Accomplishing these objectives requires that this creativity be cultivated, integrated, and managed. Therefore, an effective product development structure should enable you not only to cultivate but also to channel and control this creativity (see Figure 6–3).

Effective channeling means bounding creativity by time. For example, creativity of new product ideas is the acknowledged time devoted to exploring and articulating customer needs and wants. However, at some point, *creativity of an idea* must stop to enable unimpeded *creativity of design approaches* to occur, and so on. Unbounded creativity is another term for chaos and frustration. Bounded creativity promotes maximum contribution, personal satisfaction, and optimum product development efficiency.

An Effective Decision Process

The CEO of an insurance company summarized his product development capability in saying, "We sure are good at starting projects. We're just not very good at finishing them!" This phenomenon occurs for several reasons. First, most companies don't build effective decision points into their product development processes. As a result, appropriate information often is not available to make effective product development decisions. Second, too many people are usually involved in these key decisions. Accountability becomes defused, which causes the decision process to become too time-consuming and unresponsive.

Such was the case of the Coleman Corporation. "When the Coleman Corporation attempted to compress its product development process, they discovered that each new product required as many as 16 signatures. Says Coleman development chief Mike Farmer, 'Before, we didn't allow mistakes. We went through so many channels that no one failed. We didn't get much done though.' "[30]

Therefore, critical *decision points* (see Figure 6–4), as well as the criteria on which these decisions are based, must be included in a product development process to assure that

- All required criteria are accomplished in each phase before moving to a succeeding phase.

- Product development targets have been achieved.

- Appropriate funding and resources are available to continue the next phase of the development effort.

- The product remains within the strategic product portfolio.

Operationalizing an integrated product development structure, channeling creativity, and enabling effective decision

FIGURE 6–4

   Critical New Product Development Decision Points

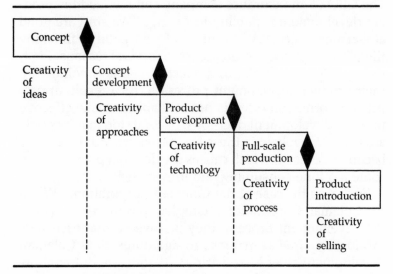

making can achieve significant cycle compression. How well can this concept work? "Coleman's revitalized new product development process cut their development time from two years to one."[31]

Integrating the Principles and the Process

Two key factors are necessary to assure competitive product development success: the principles and the process of product development. Integration of the principles and the process creates a unique way to manage and control new product development.

The process provides the *structure* for product development, whereas the principles facilitate the *discipline* necessary to understand, define, communicate, and control a product's definition. The catalyst is the product's definition. The definition is the communication link between

FIGURE 6-5

Integrating the Principles and the Process

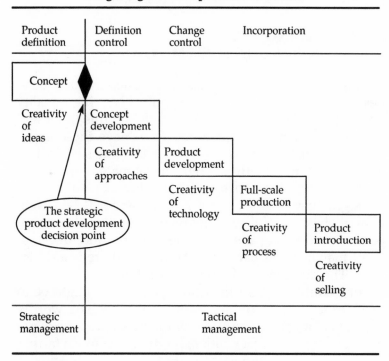

the who, what, when, why, and where of new product development.

As Figure 6-5 illustrates, a product's definition is your strategic control of the tactical phases and processes of product development. How does this work in practice?

The purpose of a product's definition is to state what the product should be. The strategic decision process must decide if it is the right product. A competitive new product development process must effectively address both variables. Once this *strategic* decision has been made, the three remaining principles—definition control, change control, and incorporation—can assure that the product definition will be accurately maintained throughout the product's *tactical* development processes.

MANAGING THE
ORGANIZATIONAL ELEMENTS

To sustain its competitiveness, a product-oriented business must continually develop innovative, high-quality products. Moreover, the business must do this faster and at less cost than its competitors. To achieve these objectives, the business must operationalize and sustain two interdependent initiatives: "right-first-time development" and "right-first-time operations" (see Figure 6–6).

"Right first time" is not a new message. It is a well-known objective of the quality revolution. It is also an important underlying theme of the new product development management paradigm. However, there is a difference. The difference is found in the intent.

For example, a right-first-time quality goal might be to produce a perfect product. Admittedly, this is a worthy objective. However, the intent of the new paradigm is not only development of a faultless product. It is much farther reaching. Equally important is the concurrent creation of a development process that promotes the product's *stability, integrity, accuracy,* and *manufacturability* (Figure 6–6A). This scenario optimizes the value and application of other initiatives such as Design For Assembly, MRPII, JIT, and Statistical Process Control.

The analysis of the Japanese/Western comparison model in Chapter Four clearly showed the value of stability, integrity, accuracy, and manufacturability on downstream operations. In turn, these development attributes enable right-first-time operations to become a reality. This is a key precept of the new paradigm. It directly links the product development and product operations processes. It is an understanding, awareness, and acknowledgement that

FIGURE 6-6

The Benefits of Right-First-Time Development and Operations

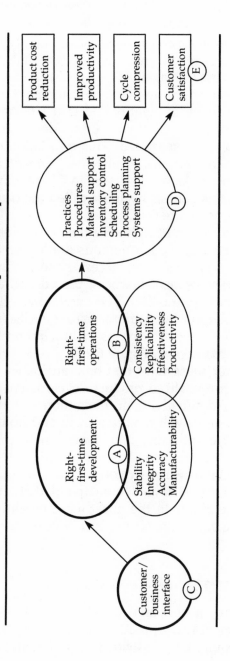

operational *consistency, replicability, effectiveness,* and *productivity* can result only from a right-first-time development process (see again Figure 6–6B).

However, right-first-time development cannot begin until the ability to identify and translate customer needs and wants into definitive product development requirements has been mastered. This translation of wants and needs is the genesis of effective product development management. As we discussed in Chapter Five, the point at which this genesis begins is called the *customer/business interface* (see Figure 6–6C).

The synergism of right-first-time development and operations creates the harmonious unification of processes, functions, and resources necessary to optimize the basic product development practices, procedures, and processes (see again Figure 6–6D). The cumulative effects of these mutually supportive attributes are *cost reduction, productivity improvement, cycle compression,* and *increased customer satisfaction opportunities* (Figure 6–6E).

Together these right-first-time attributes comprise the *intent* of a revitalized product development management process. Admittedly, their integration will not happen by intent alone. It will require a fresh and holistic approach to measure, manage, and control new product development.

However, as we've explored earlier, there are few alternatives. Others have demonstrated that the results are worth the effort. In the quest for competitiveness, there can be no substitute for product development excellence.

PDM: The Integrator's Challenge

Introducing a new and revitalized product development management (PDM) methodology is a strategic initiative. It will require businesswide integration and coordination.

The breadth of necessary cross-functional coordination and support implies understanding, vision, and leadership.

The new paradigm runs counter to the forces and intrigues of functional fiefdoms. Suboptimized perspectives, inherent within most organizations, must be overcome to set the new paradigm in motion. The import of these multiple challenges is clear. Integration, insight, and personal leadership will be critical success factors.

Therefore, operationalization of a revitalized product development management methodology requires that you, the business leader, be its integrator. The following chapters will discuss these new product development principles and innovative practices in more detail. They are your guide to mastery of the principles of the new product development paradigm.

Chapter Seven

Assuring Process Stability

I ncreasing process stability can create significant cost reduction and cycle compression opportunities. This was
clearly illustrated in Chapter Four by the analysis and
findings of the Japanese/Western comparative model. However, before you can capture the benefits of product development stability, you must first discern the *source* of
this stability. Next, you must initiate ways that can enable
your organization to sustain it.

THE SOURCE OF STABILITY

Stability is a subtle discipline. Yet at the same time it is so
powerful that once it has been experienced its absence is
immediately discomforting—like watching a movie that is
out of focus. Achieving process stability is like hovering a
helicopter.

Remember from the discussion in Chapter Three how a
pilot can hover a helicopter by mastering the integration
and balance of altitude, attitude, power, and heading?

And that if the pilot fails to balance these forces, the aircraft would become unstable and crash? Similarly, to maintain stability of your product development process, you must integrate and balance your strategic, human, technological, financial, and organizational dynamics.

The source of this stability is an early and continuous understanding of what *it* is that you intend to create. The Coleman Corporation found this to be true when its market position was attacked by competitors. To further speed development, the company set clear boundaries for new products. Explains Coleman's development chief, Mike Farmer, "We could never pound a stake in the ground and say, 'This is what I want.' We were always changing our mind and not getting anywhere." When the company set out last year to develop a new outdoor lamp, it set clear boundaries. For example, the lantern would produce 80 candlepower, use propane fuel, and be less rugged than camping lanterns. The result was that Coleman cut development time from two years to one.[32] The principle to remember is that, like the Coleman Corporation, you cannot expect your organization to develop products right the first time until you can first define what the right *it* is.

Early product definition is the source of product development stability. It is the source that "energizes" functional elements into action. A product's definition is the source for estimating the work necessary to create the product to meet that definition. It provides the basis for making strategic and tactical product decisions. It is the "enabler" of precise communication of product requirements and the "predictor" of development results.

By the same token, the clearer the product's definition is, the higher the probability will be that you can accelerate or compress the processes required to build it. Conversely, a late or fuzzy definition can create developmental dynamics such that your new product development capability can be brought to a standstill. Finally, a product's definition can be your source for measuring and delivering customer satisfaction.

THE PRODUCT DEFINITION PROCESS

An effective product definition process would be a critical success factor if you were developing only one product. Unfortunately, this is seldom the case. Today's average international company has more than 25 product/projects simultaneously in the works. Many have over 100!

This multi–product/project business environment adds even more credence to the old adage "You can't manage what you can't define." If you find yourself within this norm, operationalization of an efficient product definition process is a must. This requires fulfillment of four criteria. You must first define the product and then validate, approve, and control the product's definition throughout its life cycle.

Defining a Product

Defining a product is an iterative process. It begins by identifying customer needs and wants. It ends with the finalization of a complete product documentation package. Based on the complexity of your products, a new product's initial definition can take any form, from a simple idea statement to a detailed set of specifications. The purpose of a product's definition is to

- Communicate what *it* is that you intend to create to those who will create it.

- Provide a quantifiable basis for deciding the new product's economic, technical, and strategic potential viability.

- Coordinate and integrate the "creating elements" to achieve common cost, quality, and timing objectives.

- Authorize work or funds to be expended to produce the product.

- Provide a baseline from which achievement can be quantified and measured.

A product's definition begins the conversion of a strategic new product portfolio into reality. Its importance mandates that a product's definition be *timely, comprehensive*, and *comprehendible*. It also requires that it be *formally approved* and *controlled*. Let's discuss the rationale of these criteria in more detail.

Timely

The real purpose of a product's definition is to provide guidance and stability to those who will create it. Therefore, it should be created early in the development process, before development begins. Unfortunately, many companies choose to document what has been created already. They ask, "Why go through the hassle of defining a product and then trying to maintain this definition? Why not just wait until development is done and then document the product?" This is the ongoing controversy between *timely* and *ultimate* product definition.

Timely product definition is done early in a product's development. It is the communicative and evaluative vehicle for managing new product development. In contrast, ultimate product definition is only done to fulfill a documentation requirement.

An international computer manufacturer provides an example of the results of following an ultimate product definition philosophy. The company habitually defined and documented its products six months to a year *after* the products had been manufactured and introduced into the market. Some products that did not sell well were not documented at all! To warrant and repair these poorly documented products, the company's main service center employed 43 electrical and software engineers—just to resolve the queries that emanated from attempts to repair the undocumented products! The company's "loose" product definition and control policy cost it millions of dollars of avoidable service and repair costs each year. It also did little to increase customer satisfaction.

In another case, a computer peripheral manufacturer received a repeat order for a custom product. The company's failure to properly document the earlier product required a team of engineers and a photographer to reconstruct the product's definition at the client site. What a way to build customer confidence!

Waiting to document what *has been* created is de facto acceptance of the non-value-added costs and turbulence of change depicted by the Japanese/Western comparative model. Adoption of an ultimate product definition philosophy is an abdication by management. It is akin to surrendering to your competitors. Ultimately, it is the beginning of the end.

Comprehensive

You need not write a book of specifications to define a product. However, the level of detail should be sufficient to evaluate the product's marketing, technical, financial, and strategic feasibility. It should also communicate the needs of the intended customer. This logic is simple and straightforward, but it is seldom practiced. As a result, seemingly well-executed new product development projects too often meet unexpected and costly obstacles.

As an illustration, a pharmaceutical company initiated a program to develop a new medical device. The prototype had successfully passed several clinical evaluations, and full-scale production had begun. During the filming of a sales video, the actress portraying the intended user experienced difficulty activating the product. This unexpected problem delayed the product's introduction until the problem could be corrected. A cause of the problem was traced back to inadequate product definition. In this case, a marketing representative did not fully specify the requirements of the end user, a seriously ill patient. The marketing representative, who was just "filling in a 'required' requirement," merely assumed everyone knew the end-user's needs. Months later, this omission of a seemingly simple detail resulted in significant loss of time, added product costs, and missed revenue opportunities. Early and comprehensive product definition is a prerequisite for any successful product development capability.

Comprehendible
Napoleon knew the importance of giving clear and comprehendible orders. To test his orders' clarity, he assigned his adjutant to read each one and tell him what it meant. If the adjutant, being of average intelligence, understood the meaning of the dispatch, Napoleon was assured that his commanders would comprehend it as well.

Likewise, because a product's definition is the basis for its development "campaign," it deserves the "Napoleon's adjutant" test to assure its comprehendibility. Generally speaking, when this test does not occur, the ensuing product development process will be out of control. Not so? Just take a moment to revisit the Japanese/Western comparative model discussed in Chapter Four.

The validity of the above statement about the necessity of a comprehendible definition can also be found in the case of a transport vehicle manufacturer. Although besieged with unplanned development costs, customer requests, and schedule problems, the manufacturer was adamant that these problems were not the result of its "impeccable" product definition process. However, an analysis revealed otherwise. The manufacturer's usual practice for defining a product was to copy the customer's detailed specifications, containing hundreds of pages of "boiler plate" clauses and conditions. These copies would then be distributed to all internal functions and external subcontractors. Weeks later a familiar pattern began to emerge:

- The program manager could no longer keep the customer from making "unreasonable" product requests.

- Engineering disciplines became engaged in battles over supremacy of design approaches and the impact of unexpected design changes.

- Vendors began delivering parts and components that were incompatible with the "originally proposed" design.

- An overlooked critical calculation placed the entire design in jeopardy. It's rectification required major rework of more than 50 multimillion-dollar vehicles to meet original program compliance.

What was the source of these problems? Was it, as management believed, the inevitable result of escalating complexity of acquiring new business? Not in this case. Here, the underlying problem was a simpler one. Although everyone had a copy of the product specifications, no one had *interpreted* the customer's specifications to define the product in terms the company and its suppliers could understand. Instead, the elements were each obliged to interpret the specification for themselves. No wonder there was no stability in the manufacturer's product development process!

Formally Approved

When the future of your business is built on the success of 10, 20, or even 50 new products, a formal approval process becomes your primary means of strategically controlling your new product development effort. The basis of this approval process is the product's definition. Without it, you have no foundation for communicating, estimating, feasibility planning, allocating resources, financial planning, or ascertaining the predictability of a product's success.

Adopting this step provides an added benefit. A formal approval process will also help assure that your product definitions are accurate, timely, comprehendible, and comprehensive. This is because you cannot estimate or evaluate what you cannot understand. Nor can you approve what cannot be comprehended.

Controlled

Given the importance of a product's definition to the wellness of your entire product development process, it should be obvious that the definition must be formally controlled. Following this principle would have prevented some of the problems that caused the failure of a process control developer. Although the company was recognized as having one of the most advanced and reliable process controllers in the industry, it was forced out of business by lessor competitors. Here is why.

Customers had requested a new controller with state-of-the-art features. The company's brightest software engineers eagerly took on this challenge. For nearly three years, designers and customers added breakthrough feature after breakthrough feature. Nearly 3 million lines of code were written and rewritten. However, while the design was noteworthy and the promised completion was always in sight, the final product was never attained. The company's failure to control the definition of the new product was a prime factor in its inability to focus on the output. By continually redefining the product, the company failed to put a "stake in the sand." Instead, it allowed the state-of-the-art quest to overshadow the need to meet the company's rivals' introduction of increasingly "good enough" new products.

The purpose of all of the above examples is to cause you to rethink the role and value of a product's definition in your new product development process, to realize it is not just another administrative requirement but rather that effective management and control of product definition is the first step toward effective product development management.

Validating Your Product Definition

Whenever you define a product, you also must determine the technological, financial, and organizational capability trade-offs required to create it. The adequacy of your product definition process can be found in the answers to two key questions: How do you determine a new product's "gotta haves," and How do you determine a new product's "gonna gets"? "Gotta haves" are the requirements or features that customers, managers, or others say they want. As an example, marketing may say, "We gotta have a 486/50MH notebook computer with a 120-megabyte hard drive, active matrix color screen, built-in mouse, 4.5 hour battery life, a weight of less than 5 pounds, and a cost of less than $3,500—and we need it for the next Computer Exposition."

In contrast, "gonna gets" are a reflection of the priorities, resource availabilities, technical feasibilities, and functional capabilities as determined by management, engineering, manufacturing, materials, or others. These may take the form of a composite reply: "For $3,500 and in time for the next Computer Exposition, all you're gonna get is a prototype 386SX/25MH laptop computer with an 80-

megabyte hard drive, passive-matrix color screen; 2.5-hour battery life, and a weight of 6.5 pounds. Sorry, it's the best we can do."

The above example illustrates the obvious need for negotiation between the two sets of expectations. Unfortunately, this key activity is seldom achieved. The reason is that a product's "requirements" often are not adequately defined, evaluated, or controlled in most organizations.

The result is "creeping specs," or a "we'll-design-it-as-we-go" philosophy, both of which, we now know, can add significant cost and time to a product development cycle. The same is true for discerning an organization's product development capability. Commonly, this is engineering's technical decision rather than a comprehensive decision emanating from marketing, research and development, engineering, manufacturing, quality, procurement, facilities, and others. Too often, it is an emotional management decision or edict that may not be well-founded.

Such was the case of a high-tech office equipment manufacturer battered by its worthy competitors. At a weekend off-site meeting, the frustrated executive team conceptualized a product that, in their words, "would leave the competition standing in the dust." Unfortunately, the technology was too premature and the schedule too ambitious to meet their expectations. Even more regrettably, the project consumed so many critical resources that it precluded the introduction of several less revolutionary products that cumulatively might have made even greater revenue contributions.

Before you can establish more realistic expectations between a new product's requirements and your organizational capabilities, you must resolve the variations that will invariably exist between these two criteria. Unfortunately, most businesses do not address this issue. Instead, stated requirements that are beyond an organization's capabilities often remain as "stretch" targets that management hopes can be met during the ensuing product development.

Attempting to meet unreasonable stretch targets can add needless product development risks, generate avoidable change, and destroy morale. Following this path not only destabilizes the product development effort but also debilitates organizational productivity and negates achievement of optimal cost and schedule targets. As the leader of your business, you must take action to assure that gotta have and gonna get negotiation occurs. Few others will.

As one project manager of an impossible project explained, "If you think I'm going to tell them [the executive team] the project can't be finished 18 months from now, you're out of your mind! They don't want to hear 'it can't be done.' They'll just replace me with someone else who won't tell the truth. No, it's better to just go on and periodically slip the cost and schedule projections as usual."

Rationalizing Your Product Definition

A product's definition provides a basis for rationalizing and achieving fundamental new product planning and control objectives. These objectives are as follows:

- Determining a new product candidate's economic, technical, and strategic applicability *before* allocating critical resources for its development.

- Providing a *quantitative* planning and measurement baseline and performance feedback medium to the creating functions.

- Coordinating and integrating the organizational elements to achieve *common* cost, quality, and timing objectives.

- *Winnowing* breakthrough new products from marginal "pet" products.

These are important objectives that every competitive company must achieve. However, they will not be operationalized without a way to rationalize product proposals before you expend resources to begin their development. Implementation of this critical process involves three steps.

Step 1. *Form a cross-functional team to review each new product definition package for strategic alignment and initial feasibility.* This review provides a forum where new product ideas can continue to be expressed on an equal basis. The review enables a respected team to screen all new product candidates for economic, technical, and strategic applicability *before* allocating funds for their development. This step also ensures that critical resources will not be "energized" to produce a product that does not meet the review criteria.

Step 2. *Evaluate and negotiate the proposed products' needs, capabilities, and feasibilities.* Early and accurate evaluation and comparison of a product's requirements and capabilities enable you to define "reality" for your organization. Evaluation and negotiation enable you to decide what you technically and economically can do from what you may wish to do. This step is your means to identify and manage your strategic product portfolio risk.

Step 3. *Formally rationalize and approve or disapprove the new product request package.* Rationalization and approval together form a difficult step because they require acceptance of standard business parametrics on which all products/projects are measured. Typical parametrics might include the following:

- Return on investment.
- Technical feasibility.
- Profit margin contribution.
- Competitive advantage.

- Strategic importance.
- Revenue generation.
- Capital investment.
- Probability of success.

A formal rationalization and approval process is your pulse and control of product development. It enables you to know when you are "betting the business" (or at least a portion of it) on a promising new product. It also enables you to know when to kill a marginal, undoable, or pet product, whatever its source. Does it work? One CEO calls his company's rationalization process "my new product decision architecture for the 21st century." Another credits the concept with "saving my company." A third is using it to increase the predictability of his company's product development processes.

ORGANIZATIONAL STABILITY AND THE PRODUCT DEVELOPMENT PROCESS

An effective product development management (PDM) process begins when an entity—the end result (the *it*) you wish to achieve—has been defined. This fact cannot be overstated. A product's definition is the source that energizes functional elements to begin work; it is the drumbeat that enables functional product development support elements to get in step with each other. It enables them to define, communicate, control, and create the *it* with a high degree of predictability. Product definition is the source of stability.

Organizational stability is both a result and a continuance of the product definition process. This is because, throughout a product's development, organizational elements continually interact as providers or receivers of goods and services. Therefore, the translation of a product's definition is an iterative and ongoing process.

The translators and interpreters of the product's definition include marketing, which typically originates *it*; engineering, which designs *it*; procurement, which purchases material for *it*; manufacturing, which builds *it*; testing, which tests *it*; and other departments, which administer *it*. However, while functional elements may delineate the structure of your product development process, it is the relationship of these elements that defines its complexity. The principle here is, *The more complex or undefined these relationships, the less stable they can become and the less predictable the outputs of their interactions, that is, your new products, will be.*

This is a key, but not necessarily revolutionary, thought. Some companies have learned, and others are learning, that it pays to design and build quality into the product rather than attempting to inspect it in. For even greater economies of scale, you also must build greater stability and predictability into your product development processes.

BUILDING STABILITY INTO THE PRODUCT DEVELOPMENT PROCESS

There are several reasons why building stability into the product development process is important. First, developing a product typically involves more than one individual or organizational element. Second, positive and accurate communication is a prerequisite for successfully integrating these diverse elements. Third, product changes and new approaches will typically occur during a product's development.

Therefore, you must be able to accommodate these dynamics without having an adverse impact on organizational productivity. In essence, a stable product development process is a "no surprises" product development process. Let's apply this logic to a typical product development scenario.

If you were creating a product solely by yourself, stability would be less of an issue. You would not have to define the product to anyone. Nor would you need to communicate any product information until you were finished and the product was ready for sale. However, this is rarely the case. Today, tens to hundreds to thousands of people are involved in the development and production of a new product. As a product's development proceeds, these supporting elements must have access to product data and an effective process for "translating" the data into their respective "languages." For example,

- Engineering translates the product definition into drawings, bills of material, and component specifications.

- Manufacturing translates the product definition into tooling, fixtures, and processes.

- Material translates the product definition into product structure, part numbers, and receiving inspection criteria.

Stability is maintained when a manufactured product's *physical definition* consistently equals its *documented definition* throughout its life cycle.

Admittedly, maintaining stability is a "simple to say, difficult to do" concept. Yet it is not just another theoretical construct. There are several reasons why achieving product stability must become one of your top priorities. One reason is that it makes good economic sense. The Japanese/Western comparative model discussed in Chapter Four proves the value. Another reason is that it is an underlying intent of the international quality initiative ISO

9000. As we shall discuss further in Chapter Nine, unless your product's physical configuration consistently equals its documented definition, your ISO 9000 certification may be in doubt. If your ISO 9000 certification is in doubt, your ability to compete globally will also be in doubt.

Dependent and Independent Zones

Embedded within a product development process are zones where functions or individuals *may* act independently or *must* act dependently. These dynamics enable the creation of independent and dependant zones of development. Independent zones, as their name implies, allow the greatest autonomy and flexibility of work.

As a rule, the greatest opportunity to implement independent zones comes early in a product's development (Figure 7–1). An example might be a salesperson's direct interaction with a customer. In this *independent* relationship, each party is free to negotiate and change product requirements (within their respective authorities). However, once binding requirements or data are "released" to other elements, their relationship changes. They now enter into a *dependent* relationship with each of these elements. At this point, neither party can autonomously change this shared information without potentially impacting the other.

As Figure 7–1 illustrates, dependencies increase as the product's development progresses. In turn, an element's ability to act independently decreases. The same principle applies at the design level. In early, independent phases of design, autonomous engineers or product development teams are free to make unilateral changes (within their respective authorities) to achieve their assigned design targets.

However, once they release data or documentation to another element, they enter into a dependent relationship

FIGURE 7–1

Dependent and Independent Zones

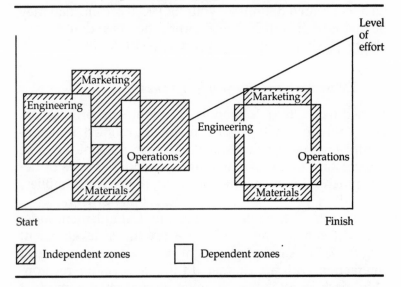

| Independent zones | Dependent zones |

with the receiving element(s). From this point forward, any changes to the released data or documentation must be coordinated with all dependent elements to prevent destabilizing or jeopardizing their work (see Figure 7–2). This is an important point. It epitomizes the "80/20" rule. This means all changes do not need to be controlled all of the time—only those that will impact *released* data or documentation.

For example, if you are writing a detailed employee handbook on your word processor, you can make as many changes to the document as you wish. You need not co-ordinate these changes with anyone. Now an associate asks for a copy of the handbook's new vacation policy to develop a presentation for new employees. What has changed? Are you still free to continue changing the handbook? The answer is yes, but with one exception. You

FIGURE 7–2

The Dynamics of Dependent Change

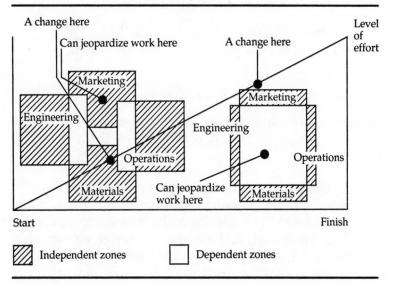

Start   Finish

Independent zones   Dependent zones

must now coordinate any vacation policy changes before you can implement or release them to others.

Without this coordination, changes will ripple through dependent elements like a domino effect, adding unnecessary cost, frustration, rework, and time to the development schedule. Independent zones provide the greatest amount of autonomy and therefore require the least amount of external coordination and control, whereas dependent zones provide the least amount of autonomy.

Dependent zones also require the most communication, coordination, and control. As a result, greater time and effort must be expended to assure that all changes are constantly coordinated with each potentially affected element. The principle to remember here is this: The more autonomous zones you can create and the longer you can sustain them,

- The greater the autonomy of effort.
- The more stable and predictable your processes.
- The lower your product development costs.
- The faster new products can be developed.

Establishing Independent Zones

System engineering plays a key role in establishing independent design zones. It accomplishes them in three steps:

1. *Decompose the product definition into system requirements.* This step assures that the product's definition is sufficient to enable the major systems to be identified, integrated, and assigned to design elements. If you can't accomplish this step with acceptable certainty, you're not ready to begin development.

2. *Delineate and allocate system requirements to the applicable design requirements.* This step is a further decomposition of the preceding step. Here, specific design requirements are allocated to specific systems. In the case of a new car, particular performance requirements might be allocated to the engine, the power train, or the chassis teams. The combined achievement of each system requirement should equal the performance targets for the vehicle. Similarly, all product development requirements must be allocated and controlled to assure predictability of product development success.

3. *Define adequate interface controls.* Defining interface controls means that the critical input, output, and other specific criteria are allocated to each system or subsystem. For example, if size and weight are critical design criteria, then the size and weight of each system or subsystem must be defined. If electrical power is another, then the type and amount of power generated or consumed (i.e., the input and output) of each system or subsystem must also be defined or at least estimated.

These critical tasks are difficult to accomplish in today's product development environment, primarily because they require key product decisions to be made early in a product's development. This is uncomfortable to some and threatening to others. The unknowns are great and the risks of error are high at this point.

However, when these tasks are done correctly, each product development team is authorized to make independent design decisions until it releases data to another element. Each product development team can act autonomously (see Figure 7–3). Each product development team is empowered. The obvious benefits of autonomous zones are the following:

- Design elements *empowered* to operate simultaneously.

- Increased *predictability* of design integration.

- *Avoidance* of frequent, time-consuming, and costly design review meetings to ensure control.

- *Minimization* of non-value-added change.

Unfortunately, most companies fail to establish autonomous zones or define effective interface controls. Instead, they choose a seemingly faster product development approach, one that provides them an illusion of progress and control. However, almost without exception, analysis of their unexpected changes, cost overruns, and

FIGURE 7–3

Creating Autonomous Design Zones

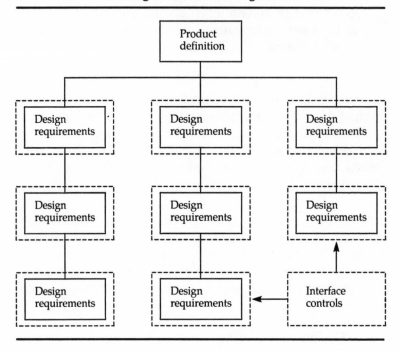

missed schedules reveals this choice to be a much more costly one (see Figure 7–4).

Figure 7–4 shows an important chart. It contrasts two product development approaches. The first approach is the typical one of "Hurry up, we're already behind schedule." The second is an approach that defines work assignments and the necessary controls *before* development begins. Let's discuss each individually.

The "Hurry-up" Approach
In this approach, because cost and schedule are the key issues, time is generally not taken to develop an adequate

FIGURE 7–4

Results of Uncontrolled Early Project Loading

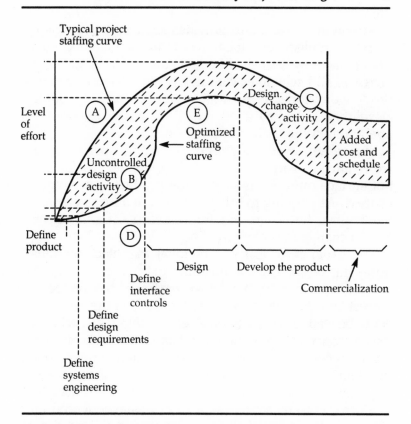

Source: This material was published by the author in *1989 Transactions of the American Association of Cost Engineers*, a publication of AACE International.

product definition, systems and design requirements, or interface controls. Advocates of "Hurry up, we're already behind schedule" believe that taking time to understand and control what they're *going to do* will only slow them down. This is represented by the typical staffing curve (Point A in Figure 7–4). As a result, individual design and functional elements begin to work in an uncontrolled, fuzzy product development environment (Point B in Figure 7–4).

Although this scenario provides an early perception of work accomplishment, it begins a familiar chain of events. Change activity escalates, budgets are overrun, meetings increase, and schedules continually slip. Then comes the product developer's lament: "*We* were ahead of schedule. Development looked good. Then see what happened in operations. Where did *they* go wrong?"

The reason everything went wrong in operations, as we've already learned, is that developmental problems do not surface until much later in the product development process. Attempting to hurry a design in a fuzzy environment gives fertile ground for unnecessary and uncontrolled change to proliferate (Point C in Figure 7–4).

The experience of a international manufacturer illustrates this point. The manufacturer discovered its best engineers were being required to remain with a project to correct "production" problems. This caused the next project to be staffed with less-experienced engineers, who followed their previous product development practices. Their inexperience again introduced even more "operational problems." As a result, the best of these engineers were required to stay on to "fix" their mistakes. This caused the next project to be staffed with even less-experienced engineers, who followed their earlier practices—and down the slippery slope they went.

The Optimized Staffing Approach

In this approach, time is taken to decompose and validate the product definition. Systems requirements and interface controls are established, and design teams are assigned (Point D in Figure 7–4). The result is an optimized staffing of critical development resources to be assigned only when needed (Point E in Figure 7–4).

Contrary to the first approach, the interface controls reduce unnecessary change activity, enabling the teams to focus on value-added effort. This reduces development costs, enhances stability, and increases the predictability of meeting development targets. More important, unlike the case of the international manufacturer, decreased change activity can enable timely redeployment of critical resources when the product development effort is done right the first time.

The results of habitually failing to establish control of early product development are as inescapable as they are unforgiving. The proof is evident in the Japanese/Western comparative model. It is evident in the aerospace/defense contractor's example. It is probably evident in your product development process. Where it is *not* evident is in the most competitive companies.

Product Development Management (PDM): The Key to Process Stability

The key to successfully stabilizing your new product development processes is the adoption of a revitalized product development management (PDM) philosophy. As we have previously discussed, assuring effective product definition control in the early phases of product development can result in the following:

- Plateaus of stability providing significant opportunities to further compress product development cycles.

- Enhanced product integrity to promote process stability and facilitate achievement of aggressive quality, reliability, and maintainability objectives.

- Fewer changes and associated costs introduced into the design and process functions.

- Greater predictability of accurately translating the product's definition into documentation, material, and processes.

- Successful ISO 9000 verification and certification.

The net result of an effective PDM methodology is greater stability and predictability of your product development processes. In turn, achieving these objectives will reduce unnecessary and avoidable change. In turn, this key success factor can enable other important initiatives such as computer-aided design, just-in-time, simultaneous engineering, manufacturing resource planning, computer-integrated manufacturing, and quality management to work more efficiently.

Chapter Eight
Effectively Managing Product Change

I n Chapter Seven we discussed how stability of a product development process can minimize unnecessary
change. But no matter how well we plan or design, we
should anticipate product change. It will occur in the most
well-engineered products. Change is a necessary part of
life. It's the reason pencils have erasers and computer key-
boards have delete keys.

At the same time, change must be managed to avoid
disrupting the efficiency of the functional elements assigned to create the product. This doesn't mean managing
only the *major* product changes, such as adding or deleting
a product feature; the hundreds or thousands of *minor*
product changes must be addressed as well. It is the
cumulative effect of *all* these changes that can debilitate
operational performance. Left uncontrolled, they can rob

you of millions of potential profit dollars and an irreplaceable resource—time. Hence, your competitiveness may depend on how well *you manage and control all product change*.

TWO CHANGE
MANAGEMENT MYTHS

Before discussing the characteristics of effective product change management, we need to debunk two myths most often quoted as reasons to avoid managing product change. The first myth is that control can be regained by "freezing the design." This last-ditch change management strategy is usually invoked during the final stages of product development. It's nothing more than an edict to stop further changes to a product's design.

The second myth is that change management prevents or unacceptably impedes continuous product improvement. The purpose of continuous improvement (CI) is, as its name implies, to continually improve a product and its development processes. Unfortunately, more often than not, continuous improvement prevents these objectives from being realized. The reason is, most people fail to understand, that continuous improvement is merely another term for change.

Freezing the Design

Admittedly, change management is often as frustrating as it is necessary. This is particularly true when a product's development is out of control. Yet what can you do when faced with this situation? Too often, management reverts to dire and unworkable measures to regain control. Freezing the design is such a measure.

While freezing the design may appease the emotions of the moment, it does little to solve the real problem—uncontrolled change. Freezing the design is an emotional reaction, *not* a logical solution. The reason is simple. When you decide to freeze a design, you're making several key assumptions:

(1) *The product is acceptable as designed.* If the design is not acceptable, does it make sense to freeze it?

(2) *All components and systems "fit" and "function" as designed or required.* If the fit and function of components or systems are not acceptable, does it make sense to freeze an unacceptable design?

(3) *There are no outstanding change requests to be considered.* If there are outstanding change requests that have not been put into action, what do you do with these changes? If there are changes outstanding, does it make sense to freeze the design?

Few developers can affirm that these assumptions have been met, yet many still believe that freezing the design is a viable strategy. A chief automotive engineer was a follower of such a philosophy. During the development of a new model car, he was asked, "How do you manage the design of the car?"

He replied, "I purposely have not imposed many controls. I want my designers to be free to make the changes they feel are necessary to create a world-class car. [Another example of fuzzy thinking!] When we get closer to production, I'll freeze the design. From that point forward no more changes will be allowed."

A review of the automobile company's product development environment helps put the chief engineer's comments and strategy into perspective:

- The car was in the final year of development.

- Responsibility for the car's design was allocated among 13 business teams and more than 80 product development teams.

- There were no approved Level 1 specifications or interface controls to coordinate and guide the efforts of these product development teams.

- No centralized change scheduling, tracking, or management reporting system was available to support the development effort.

- Over 2,400 outstanding change requests were awaiting review or actioning.

The above represents a case where freezing the design was not an appropriate strategy for several reasons. First, the chief engineer failed to establish interface controls, autonomous design zones, or basic controls for his product development teams. As a result, his invitation to "make all the changes necessary to create a world-class car" led to an environment of widespread interpretation and uncontrolled change.

Second, his decision to "wait until production" before attempting to control product change destabilized the entire product development process. Moreover, it severely impacted production and assembly operations. Imagine the chaos that might be experienced within manufacturing if the expectation of a frozen design was simultaneously accompanied by 2,400 unpredicted changes!

Third, the chief engineer did not have adequate change scheduling, tracking, or management information on which to base his decision to freeze the design. As a result, he was unaware of the magnitude of outstanding change requests.

Is this product development scenario atypical? Unfortunately, it is not. This scenario fits too well the Western profile in the Japanese/Western comparative model. It means too many product development processes are being managed with this "seat-of-the-pants" design freeze mentality. Remember, a design freeze is not a viable change management strategy *unless* you have a high degree of assurance that the "as-is" design is acceptable and manufacturable, and that there are no design changes pending. In contrast, if the design is acceptable and manufacturable, and there are no pending or unactioned design changes, is there a reason to freeze it?

Continuous Improvement (CI)

Continuous improvement is currently being touted as "the way" to improve business performance. Its purpose is to stimulate corporate "creative think" to generate innovative ways of designing a product or improving the processes to develop it. Used appropriately, the potential contributions of CI are endless. At the same time, this method has prevented well-intentioned businesses from achieving their objectives. A primary reason is that *continuous improvement* is another term for *change*. Admittedly, while well-directed change may improve an operation, it also destabilizes it. As such, all continuous improvement initiatives, like all product change, must be managed.

Unfortunately, many managers have not developed an ability to discern or visualize how new methodologies such as continuous improvement really work. As a result, they often falsely assume that adoption of CI is a license to eliminate or reduce "restrictive" change controls. When this occurs, adequate control of continuous improvement initiatives is lost, not to mention the development of new products as well.

A case example illustrates this point. The manager of a $100 million product development project enthusiastically encouraged his team to think and practice continuous improvement. When later questioned about how the continuous improvement initiative might impact the success of his project, he had no answer. In his zest to create the best new product, he overlooked three simple and unrelenting continuous improvement principles:

- Operationalizing continuous improvement ideas creates "change dynamics."

- The introduction of change dynamics must be managed to prevent destabilization.

- Continuous improvement creativity must be bound by time to maintain stability and predictability of each product development process.

To illustrate this point, let's review an earlier case example—our international carmaker. In their quest to develop the best car, the members of the project management team failed to visualize how their unbounded continuous improvement strategy would impact the overall car development processes. Now, with our greater level of awareness, it should be obvious that the ability to generate continuous improvements has limits. For example, continuous improvements within the features list must either cease or be controlled when the car systems development phase begins (see Figure 8–1).

This is not to say that great improvement ideas should not continue to be considered. They should. However, they must also be evaluated for their potential cost, sched-

FIGURE 8–1

**Case Study Example: Controlling Continuous
Improvement**

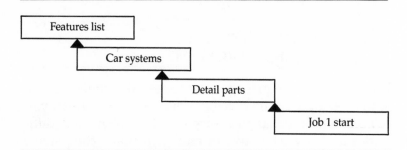

ule impact, and perceived customer value *before* being
implemented. This means that you must have an effective
change control process in place to understand and evaluate the impact of CI initiatives to assure that (1) further
change will not significantly debilitate or jeopardize other
product development effort, and (2) the cost of CI is not
greater than its value-added benefits.

A key to unlocking the myths of a design freeze or continuous improvement philosophy is to answer one question: Does this initiative increase or decrease the predictability and stability of my product development process?
The answer will no doubt reveal that neither initiative
should be used in place of an effective change management methodology. Doing otherwise only creates an illusion of control. In contrast, effective change management
offers true predictability and control. But the critics of
change management do have a point—there is a price to
pay.

Effective change management requires greater levels of
organizational understanding, discipline, and commitment.
Not just from the doers but from every member of the
management team as well. In choosing which path to fol-

low, one fact remains clear: The prize is worth the price. The proven benefits are too important to leave to the consequences of yesterday's myths.

DO YOU HAVE A CHANGE MANAGEMENT PROBLEM?

The law of change management states that whenever two or more people are involved in developing a product, you *will* encounter a change management problem. The difficulties magnify when two or more functions, companies, or countries form a partnership to develop a product. Two simple yet creative techniques can reveal whether you are experiencing a change management problem: the *temperature check* and the *periodicity profile*.

The Temperature Check

For hundreds of years, the practice of monitoring a patient's temperature has provided an accurate measure of health. The same procedure can be used to determine the wellness of a business. However, like a medic, one of the first lessons you must discern is where to stick the thermometer.

For most manufacturing operations, the point at which measurement should be taken is *kit issue*. This is where the materials needed to fabricate or assemble a product are kitted and issued. Think about it. At kit issue, all necessary product documentation, material, process planning, and workmanship practices come together to build the product.

To take your "organizational temperature," initiate a 100 percent audit of your material kit issues. To provide meaningful data, you should continue this audit for several weeks. The audit should also be accomplished by a disinterested third party, such as a quality assurance department or a specially selected audit team. To perform the audit, you need information about the following:

- Kits scheduled by date and quantity.
- Kits available for issue by date and quantity.
- Kits issued by date and quantity.
- Kit shortages and reason.
- Wrong parts issued and reason.
- Currency and accuracy of kit pick lists.
- Changes approved and not incorporated.
- Current and accurate planning documentation.

The data from the audit can enable one of the following conclusions to be reached:

(1) If 100 percent of the necessary materials are available in exactly the right quantity and type required, the bill of material is 100 percent accurate, the planning documentation is 100 percent appropriate, the documented practices are 100 percent correct, and 100 percent of these kits are issued on schedule, then you probably do not have a change management problem.

(2) On the other hand, if the necessary material is not 100 percent available or exactly as required to build the product, the bill of material is not 100 percent accurate, the planning documentation is not 100 percent correct, and 100 percent of the kits are not issued on schedule, then you probably do have a change management problem.

The temperature check can also provide an indication of the wellness of your product development and manufacturing operations. For example, suppose that all supporting processes are 100 percent accurate, correct, and on time at kit issue and that you still have a product *build* problem. In this case, the barriers and opportunities to achieve right-first-time operations are probably within operation's area of influence.

Conversely, if these supporting processes are not 100 percent accurate, correct, or on time at kit issue, then you should focus on your product *development* process. Thus, you can quickly diagnose and segregate the causes from the symptoms. As such, the temperature check is a powerful tool for providing accurate feedback on your path toward developing a capability for right-first-time development and right-first-time operations.

The Periodicity Profile

Measuring the magnitude of change activity is paramount to determining whether your organization is experiencing a change management problem. However, the magnitude of change activity provides only a one-dimensional view. Several other parameters also must be analyzed to more fully determine the true scope of any change management problem.

The purpose of the *periodicity profile* is to provide a visual perspective of both a product's change profile and the relationship of these changes to other critical factors of the product's development. These other factors are the product's drawing release schedule and the phases of its development. Together, they can illustrate the adequacy of your product development management process.

The periodicity profile begins with a simple yet powerful three-step modeling exercise, illustrated in Figure 8–2:

FIGURE 8–2

Completing the Periodicity Profile

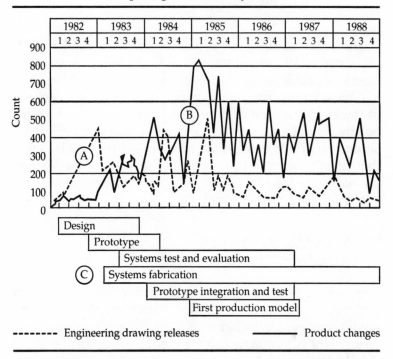

-------- Engineering drawing releases   ———— Product changes

Source: This material was prepared by the author and published in *1990 Annual Reliability and Maintainability Symposium Proceedings*. Used with permission of the Institute of Electrical and Electronics Engineers, Inc.

Step 1. Plot engineering's drawing release schedule for a recently completed or nearly completed new product (Point A in Figure 8–2).

Step 2. Overlay the product's change history. This can be accomplished by determining the number of changes initiated for this product per month (Point B in Figure 8–2).

Step 3. From the project schedule, plot when the key development milestones required to cre-

ate the product were achieved (Point C in
Figure 8–2).

The value of this type of analysis is that it quickly enables you to successfully uncover significant change management problems that often remain undetected because,
like most companies, yours is probably more accustomed
to tracking change *data* than change *information*. The periodicity model enables you to create a cause-and-effect relationship of this data—a visual snapshot that enables further investigation to be much more focused and effective.
The key is to integrate typical change data into a more visual and meaningful format.

MANAGING VERSUS
ADMINISTERING CHANGE

The control of product change generally falls within two
philosophical categories: change management and change
administration. As its name implies, the purpose of *change
management* is to *manage* value-added product change while
simultaneously *reducing* the introduction of non-value-
added change. As a result, effective change management
promotes predictability and stability of the product development processes.

In contrast, *change administration* is merely a process to
account for product change. In most instances, this approach merely assures all the *i*'s are dotted and all the *t*'s
are crossed. It does little to reduce the number or the effects of change.

However, because several of the same processes are
used within each methodology, it is often difficult to dis-
tinguish between the two. Without this awareness, one
cannot fully appreciate the *value* of change management
or understand the *limitations* of change administration. As

a result of this lack of awareness, the management of change is rarely employed

- To provide cost and schedule product change feedback to enable organizational "learning" to occur.

- As a source of business intelligence to identify product deficiencies, potential new product opportunities, product cost reduction trends, or the impact of change on functional effectiveness.

- As a discipline to compress new product development cycles; improve customer satisfaction; reduce product costs; and improve quality, reliability, and maintainability targets.

The following table can enable you to determine whether you are employing a change management (CM) or a change administration (CA) methodology.

Is Your Change System Used As:	CM	CA
A system to centralize all product change requests?	•	•
A centralized screening of all product change requests to engineering and, more specifically, the respective designer?	•	
A source of "product intelligence" for the entire management team?	•	
A source for tracking the status of change requests and change orders from their receipt through their incorporation?	•	•
A source for evaluating the comprehensive cost of change?	•	
An efficient, responsive, and proactive method to action all product change requests?	•	
An efficient, responsive, and proactive method to evaluate all change orders before they are approved?	•	

Analyzing Your Change Process

If you decide to analyze your change process, where should you begin? Typically, the analysis should start at the point where all product change requests are received and actioned. *Actioning* is the process of screening, rejecting, approving, or holding a change for a later decision. Conducting the analysis in this manner assumes that you have a centralized collection center and a system to input and manage the screening of your change requests. A good technique for evaluating the effectiveness of a collection and actioning process is to find the answers to the following questions:

- Is there a process to account for all change requests?

- Is there an adequate system for tracking change activity (e.g., requests received and their status)?

- Are change requests screened for completeness, reason, and source?

- Are rejected change requests returned to the initiator with the reason for rejection?

- On average, how much time is taken to screen a change request?

- What percentage of change requests are converted to change orders?

- Is there an adequate change control staff to accommodate the change activity?

The results of the analysis can indicate the wellness of your change management processes. For example, the faster a mandatory change request can be screened, the fewer the products that may require rework or scrapping. In another case, if all change requests are converted to change orders your organization may have a "rubber-stamp," rather than a change management, mentality.

SCREENING CHANGE REQUESTS

Hospital emergency rooms screen patients based on their urgency of need. Likewise, all businesses also should employ a triage process to screen the urgency of their product change needs. Experience shows that many change requests are based on misunderstanding, are unnecessary, or are simply inappropriate. Screening will disclose these request categories before valuable effort is expended on them.

To maximize effectiveness, two screening principles should be followed. First, screening should be done as early as possible. Second, it must always be accomplished by a qualified review element. Typically, the review element should be a team composed of "cross-functional disciplines." This screening approach achieves three key objectives:

- It assures that inappropriate changes are eliminated from the pipeline before they bring about unnecessary processing costs.

- It expedites the change management process by reducing the number of change requests that require further actioning.

- By providing rapid response and feedback, early screening guarantees that the change request pipeline remains open to continuous product improvement suggestions.

An effective screening of change requests can be one of your most effective initiatives to reduce product cost, com-

FIGURE 8–3

Change Screening Opportunities

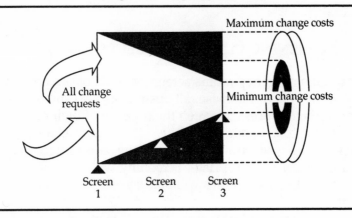

press development, and improve quality. Effective screening can enable you to identify cost-reduction opportunities while avoiding unnecessary change costs. In contrast, the failure to adequately screen product change requests will cause you to incur maximum product costs (see Figure 8–3). The three screens required to capture these benefits are described below.

Screen 1: Reduce the number of change requests. The purpose of this screen is to segregate the *essential* from the *nonessential* change requests (see Figure 8–4). A request to drill a missing hole to accommodate a cable routing would be considered an essential change request, whereas a change request based on a machine operator's inability to correctly read tolerances in the product documentation might be a nonessential change request. Adopting new drawing standards or operator training might be a more appropriate way of holistically correcting the latter request.

FIGURE 8–4
The First Screen: Reduce the Number of Requests

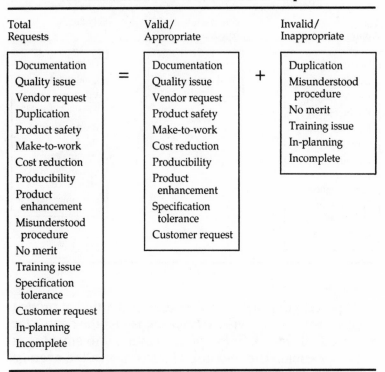

Total Requests		Valid/ Appropriate		Invalid/ Inappropriate
Documentation		Documentation		Duplication
Quality issue	=	Quality issue	+	Misunderstood procedure
Vendor request		Vendor request		No merit
Duplication		Product safety		Training issue
Product safety		Make-to-work		In-planning
Make-to-work		Cost reduction		Incomplete
Cost reduction		Producibility		
Producibility		Product enhancement		
Product enhancement		Specification tolerance		
Misunderstood procedure		Customer request		
No merit				
Training issue				
Specification tolerance				
Customer request				
In-planning				
Incomplete				

Screen 2: Reduce the disruptive effects. Segregate the valid/appropriate requests into *schedulable* or *nonschedulable* categories (see Figure 8–5). Requests for producibility and product improvement changes should be considered as schedulable, while product safety or work stoppage requests would be nonschedulable or emergency requests.

An aerospace/defense contractor provides an excellent example of the value of this screen. From a cursory perspective, the contractor had an excellent change manage-

FIGURE 8–5
The Second Screen: Reduce the Disruptive Effects

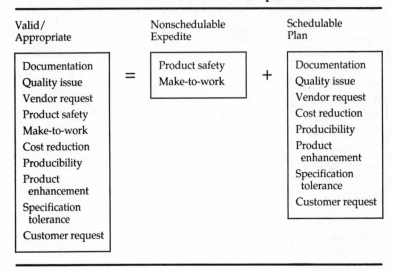

Valid/ Appropriate		Nonschedulable Expedite		Schedulable Plan

Documentation
Quality issue
Vendor request
Product safety
Make-to-work
Cost reduction
Producibility
Product
  enhancement
Specification
  tolerance
Customer request
	=	Product safety
		Make-to-work
			+	Documentation
				Quality issue
				Vendor request
				Cost reduction
				Producibility
				Product
				  enhancement
				Specification
				  tolerance
				Customer request

ment process in place. However, under scrutiny, it proved to be a costly one as well. The reason is that the contractor managed all change in the same manner: implement it as fast as possible. The measure of success was the average number of days required to process change. However, by simply following the philosophy of this screening technique and more appropriately scheduling "schedulable change," the contractor was able to avoid over 80 man-years of manufacturing rework alone!

Screen 3: Reduce the processing time. The longer it takes to action a change request, the more effort, parts, product costs, and schedules are jeopardized. Therefore, the purpose of this final screen is to segregate change requests for actioning by the lowest-level appropriate actioning authority. The importance of this screen will be discussed later in this chapter.

BUSINESS/PRODUCT INTELLIGENCE

Screening is also a valuable source of strategic business intelligence that can convert product change into new product opportunities. This can be achieved by identifying the *sources* and *reasons* for your product change requests.

Sources

The source of change shows where the request originated. Knowing the source of change is particularly helpful in identifying specific product development problems or trends. For example,

- *Requests from customers* may suggest potential problems with the current product, identify ways to improve or extend the life of a product, or signal the approaching end of a product's acceptability.

- *Requests from sales and marketing* may indicate "feature creep" as a way of enhancing a product's marketability or mask the need for a new product.

- *Requests from engineering* may indicate an inadequate design approach, a design that was released too quickly, a lack of systems integration, or a lack of design control.

- *Requests from materials* may show material or component specifications that cannot be met by suppliers, or poor quality control of product documentation.

- *Requests from manufacturing* may suggest producibility difficulties, unexpected tolerance buildup, incompatibility between engineering requirements and manufacturing capabilities, or inadequate manufacturing input prior to release of the design.

Reasons

The reason for a change tells why the request was originated. Therefore, understanding the reason for a change is an important aid in identifying potential areas for product development improvement. Reasons should be categorized by the following:

- *Product safety* is the most urgent reason for change. Lives may be threatened, or corporate wellness may be at risk. However, while changes in this category are the most critical, they also should be the fewest in number.

- *Make-to-work* means the product doesn't work as designed and immediate intervention is required. These types of changes are potential line stoppers.

- *Customer request* means the change is initiated by the customer and requires a responsive and reasoned reply.

- *Producibility* means a component, assembly, or product cannot be fabricated or assembled according to its applicable documentation or acceptable workmanship practices.

- *Cost reduction* is a recommendation that might reduce the cost of a product's development or production.

- *Product enhancement* identifies potential opportunities to improve an existing product's performance or capabilities.

- *Other (or miscellaneous)* is a category for capturing

all other reasons not otherwise identified. If this
category represents a large number of changes,
you may want to reallocate or further define your
categories.

Understanding the reasons for change is important for
several purposes. First, all changes are not alike. Therefore, the reason for a change can suggest its relative urgency. For example, product safety and make-to-work
requests are inherently immediate and nonschedulable
types of change. As such, they should receive priority
over schedulable change requests.

Second, the reason for a change provides a "reality
check" on its costs. For example, you should not spend
more for a cost reduction or product improvement change
than a reasonable return on investment (ROI) would suggest. You also may wish to negotiate reimbursement for a
customer-originated change when your product is within
its defined product specification.

To continue your change management analysis, charter
a team to screen a representative sample of schedulable
change orders. Compare the processing, rework, scrap,
and other costs of these changes against their respective
ROIs. If the change control process is working effectively,
the costs of change should be less than the ROI expected
to make the change.

ACTIONING AND COMMUNICATING A CHANGE REQUEST

Once a request for change has been properly screened, it
must be actioned. Actioning means that each change request must be defined in sufficient detail to enable the
change to be evaluated, rejected or approved, and finally
implemented. This is not a simple task.

While we might appreciate the difficulty of *designing* a product right the first time, few appreciate how difficult it is to *change* a product right the first time. As a rule, change is actioned in the manner in which products are designed. For example, if engineers design products in a vacuum, they will process change in a vacuum.

As a result, one change often causes others to occur. Corporate experience reveals that at the aggregate level, *each approved change request generates an average of .2 to .7 additional changes.* This "change-begetting-change" phenomenon is typically caused by improper actioning of a change request.

Actioning a change request can occur in one of two ways, *before* or *after* the fact. Actioning a change before the fact enables you to identify its cost and schedule effects *before* you approve it. In contrast, companies that action after the fact merely account for the cost and schedule impacts of change *after* they have been incurred.

This is an excellent example of the difference between *change management* and *change administration*. After-the-fact actioning is the most costly and disruptive method of change (I hate to use the word) management. The reason is as subtle as it is important: Many product changes would not be approved if their true impacts on cost, scheduling, and return on investment were known *before* they were actioned.

EXPEDITING THE CHANGE PROCESS

In the case of product change, time equals money. The longer it takes to action a change, the more work, material, or product must be scrapped, reworked, or dispositioned. For example, assume that you are producing 100 widgets a day and that it takes an average of 10 days to process a change. In this scenario, you would produce 1,000 widgets from the time you discovered the need for a change until the change was actioned! How much scrap or rework costs could be saved if the change actioning time could be expedited by 25 percent?

100 widgets per day × 10 days = 1,000 × .25 = 250 widgets saved from change

If the change required 20 hours of rework at $25 per hour standard cost, the savings would be:

250 widgets × 20 man-hours = 5,000 man-hours

This is equivalent to a 2.5 man-year, or $125,000, cost savings opportunity!

Remember, this example represents the potential savings of only one change. If yours is an average company, you are probably experiencing over 300 changes monthly. Therefore, your cumulative cost savings could be significantly more.

THE ELEMENTS OF CHANGE MANAGEMENT

Change management is generally accomplished via a change control board (CCB). Although a good concept, the CCB is also where the change management process most often breaks down. The reason lies not in the concept, but in its execution. CCBs typically operate outside the normal management process. This "out-of-sight, out-of-mind" condition causes several things to occur:

- Management quickly becomes out of touch with the realities of change.
- When a management vacuum exists, the CCB becomes either an autonomous bureaucracy or an administrative "rubber stamp."

- When management attention declines, the quality and morale of the CCB membership follows suit.

- Change actioning becomes backlogged, causing costly delays.

This scenario encourages the formal system to be bypassed and encourages uncontrolled change activity to occur. As this situation continues to develop, it reaffirms management's perception that change control is a costly administrative impediment to achieving a competitive product development process. It also fuels the argument that a formal change system is a process to avoid if you want to reduce cost and expedite change. Restoring the simplicity, responsiveness, and efficiency of your change control board is essential to reverse these perceptions.

COMPRESSING CHANGE MANAGEMENT

Compressing the time and effort required to manage change is the role of the third screen mentioned earlier. The purpose of this final screen is to segregate change requests for actioning by the most appropriate actioning authority. Actioning a change at the lowest appropriate level is the most effective way to compress the change management process (see Figure 8–6). This requires delegation of the requisite decision authority to action a change.

For example, A properly actioned change that does not exceed $5,000 or impact the product development schedule might be approved by a product development team leader. Another properly actioned change that exceeds $5,000 but is less than $15,000, and does not impact the product development schedule more than one week, might be approved by the project manager. All changes exceeding these parameters might be approved by a change control board chaired by a member of the executive team.

FIGURE 8–6
The Third Screen: Reduce the Time to Action a Change

Schedulable Plan	Product Development Team Leader	Product Manager	CCB
	($0–$5,000) (0 days)	($5,000–$15,000) (0–5 days)	($15,000+) (5+ days)
Documentation			
Quality issue			
Vendor request	Documentation	Quality issue	Product enhancement
Cost reduction	Vendor request	Cost reduction	
Producibility	Specification tolerance	Producibility	
Product enhancement		Customer request	
Specification tolerance			
Customer request			

This change management methodology assures that

- All changes will be properly actioned and controlled.

- All changes will be approved by the most appropriate management level.

- The actioning of change will be expedited according to its relative cost, schedule, and organizational impact.

- Change control will be maintained as a management responsibility, not another overhead function.

A New Change Control Board Methodology

Throughout this chapter, we've discussed reasons and ways to move away from traditional change administration to a change management approach. Therefore, if management of change is an expectation of management, doesn't it make sense that a CCB should be represented by managers rather than administrators? Only management representation can offer a "one-stop" change process in lieu of the time-consuming communication and decision loops inherent in most CCB operations.

As an example, an electronics manufacturer was experiencing an increasing number of change requests. Like most companies, this manufacturer's CCB was staffed by a number of engineering, manufacturing, and cost administrators. When the number of changes exceeded 600 per month, the resources of the change control board became overtaxed. Management's answer to the CCB's growing backlog and workload complaints was to work weekends if necessary. However, it quickly became apparent that a more innovative approach would be needed to overcome the CCB staff's backlog. The answer was a technical review board (TRB), which was composed of mechanical, electrical, manufacturing, and software engineering management. The TRB's role was to review all change requests before they went to the CCB.

Although nearly overwhelmed by the task, the TRB initiated a Pareto analysis of the causes of change. Surprisingly, the TRB discovered that much of the change resulted from uncoordinated policies and practices within their direct control. In less than 90 days, they successfully reduced the number of changes to fewer than 200. More important, they removed much of the *causes* of change as well. This case example reveals an important principle of change management: Change boards can *schedule* costs incurred by change; only management can *prevent* or *control* them.

Evaluating the effectiveness of your change control board should be an essential element of your change management analysis. There is no better place to begin to understand the complexity and experience they need to control the impact of change. The following questions can guide your analysis of this area:

(1) What is the backlog of change requests to be actioned?

(2) What is the average processing time needed to convert a change request to change order?

(3) Are cost and schedule impacts evaluated before or after approving a change?

(4) Are changes properly scheduled to minimize cost and schedule disruptions within the supporting functions?

(5) Are the change orders received at the functional level planned or unplanned?

(6) Are change order instructions easily comprehendible by users?

(7) Are actual change cost and schedule impacts accrued to a specific change?

(8) Do normal product development management systems such as MRPII, Purchasing, and Drawing Release systems, have the capability to adequately accommodate the existing rate of change?

(9) What specific functional-level problems (scrap, rework, understanding, etc.), result from the rate of change experienced?

EVALUATING COST MANAGEMENT OF CHANGE CONTROL

Change is inherent within any new product development process. As such, no successful business can ignore it. The key is to properly manage it, not acquiesce to it.

Experience has proven that most companies can save millions of dollars by following two simple steps. First, estimate and track your *estimated* and *actual* change costs. Second, identify and measure the impact of these changes on functional schedules.

As the largest manufacturer of a computer peripheral discovered, change management works when it is properly used. For years, the company had encouraged its sales force to routinely customize standard products to accommodate customer requests. A maximum of $150 per change was "occasionally" billed back to the purchaser for this service. These "costs of sales" were believed to be negligible. However, while this strategy may have met management's goal of being responsive to customer needs, there was little awareness of the real costs of the product changes that resulted. An analysis revealed some startling facts. These seemingly insignificant product changes resulted in an annual loss of over $7 million!

Like the company in this example, most organizations rarely capture the cost of change, on the pretext that it is too time-consuming or not cost-effective. However, they overlook the fact that *every* change has an administrative processing cost. *Every* change has an impact within some organizational function. Cumulatively, these hundreds or thousands of changes can destroy organizational productivity and require additional overhead staff to process, assimilate, and compensate for their effects. Ultimately, this non-value-added activity increases the cost and schedule of every product you produce.

EVALUATING THE CHANGE MANAGEMENT OPERATING SYSTEM

To assure that necessary change information is readily available, you need an effective change management operating system, one that is capable of accounting for, tracking, and statusing all change requests, from initial receipt to final incorporation. Except in the case of small companies with minimal change activity, the management of this amount of data requires an automated approach.

The following are suggestions of data elements and information that should be monitored:

- Origin date of the change request.
- Date the change request was received and entered into the system.
- Source code (C = customer, M = manufacturing, E = engineering, P = procurement, etc.).
- Reason code (S = safety, P = producibility, M = make work, C = cost reduction, etc.).
- Product affected.
- Change manager.
- Action code (A = accept, R = reject, H = hold).
- Action date.
- Change milestone schedule.
- Change milestone responsibility.
- Cost estimate (man-hours and material dollars).
- Actual cost (man-hours and dollars).
- Change order status (A = approved, D = disapproved, H = hold).
- Status date.
- Drawing number causing change.
- Cause code.
- Incorporation point (planned and actual).
- Effectivity point (planned and actual).

With this level of detail in a data base, the following reports can be produced to provide feedback to project, design engineering, executive, and functional management. This information also provides previously hidden sources of strategic business intelligence. For example,

- A *quantity of change by product, source, and reason* report can reveal which products are experiencing the greatest amount of change, from where, and why.

- An *average change processing time* report enables you to take action where required to compress your change management process. Remember, excessive change processing time can mean added costs and missed opportunities.

- An *aging* report identifies bypassed or other change requests that have fallen through cracks in the process. The report should also flag when your change management practices revert from a FIFO (first-in, first-out) to a FISH (first-in, still-here) philosophy.

- A *change request to change order conversion* report evaluates the effectiveness of your screening processes. For example, if you are approving 100 percent of all change requests, you're probably not screening properly. In another case, if there are no producibility, cost reduction, or product improvement change requests, you may be missing major cost saving opportunities.

- An *actual versus estimated cost* report provides an excellent training opportunity for improving cost estimating. If you can't accurately estimate a change to an existing product, how much faith can you place on estimates of a new product idea?

- An *actual versus estimated schedule* report monitors your planning ability in the same way that the cost report monitors your estimating skills.

- A *cost of change by function* report enables you to "see" the true cost of change on critical human, material, rework, and other product development resources.

- An *automated performance* report transforms change management performance to a routine and manageable process.

CHANGE MANAGEMENT AND ORGANIZATIONAL LEARNING

In most companies, change management data bases and reporting systems are very rudimentary, if they exist at all. Manual logs are the most frequently found method of administration. Most of these systems do not provide the level of detail needed for adequate control and management of change requests. Virtually none track a change past the point of its approval to assure that it has been incorporated as planned.

More important, few data bases provide feedback to project, executive, design engineering, product management, and others concerning their impact on a product's development. Without this feedback loop, you cannot learn from your experiences. Unless your organization has an ability to learn, you will always do what you've always done, and always get what you've always gotten. Given the escalating level of competitiveness, tomorrow's businesses cannot stop learning today's lessons.

Chapter Nine

Product Integrity and Customer Satisfaction

What is product integrity, and why is it a factor in determining the success of a product's development? A product's integrity is both the result and the measure of how well its development process is being or has been controlled. For example, during development, integrity means that all supporting elements have access to the latest version of a product's data. It also means that anywhere in the development cycle, a product's physical configuration and characteristics equal its documented configuration and characteristics. Unlike the aerospace contractor's periodicity profile model, integrity is synonymous with a "no-surprises" product development approach. It can also be a predictor of customer satisfaction.

As customers, most of us have experienced the results of product integrity. Unfortunately, it is much easier to discern the lack of product integrity rather than its presence. For example, remember when

- You tried to assemble your child's widget on Christmas Eve and found that the components in the box—the fragile and unique ones required to finish the widget—were either different from or not included in the directions?

- The driver's manual for your new car covered how to set the time and preset the radio stations for every model except yours?

- You unpacked your new computer and the only start-up instructions read, "Insert disk 1 in drive A and disk 2 in drive B," and your computer only had one disk drive?

- The first week at your new company when your administrative assistant was on vacation and the organizational charts, internal telephone directory, and policies and procedures in your credenza didn't match those of the "real world"?

On the flip side, product integrity has made McDonald's one of the world's most successful franchises. Whether you're in Moscow, London, Boston, or Seattle, you know your Big Mac, Coke, fries, and smiling service will be the same. In essence, product integrity means that you can expect a product to be consistent time after time after time.

A computer industry acronym describes product integrity: WYSIWYG—What you see is what you get. However, WYEIWYG—What you expect is what you get—might be a more apt description of product integrity's role in product development and the level of satisfaction your customers receive. The key for maintaining product integrity is a methodology called *change incorporation*.

CHANGE INCORPORATION

Change is only an intent until it is planned and implemented, hence the role of the fourth discipline of the new product development management model: *change incorporation*. Incorporation is the operationalization of change.

However, this change finale is much easier to articulate than to achieve because of the breadth of coordination that is required. This is because even the simplest change requires detailed planning and coordinated effort from nearly every supporting element. A myriad of inter- and intrafunctional details must be identified and integrated to assure that a change can be accommodated. For instance,

- Engineering must design the "fix."

- Purchasing must provide the materials.

- Vendors may require additional time to internally process the change.

- Production engineering may need to implement process and planning changes.

- Marketing might require a new product introduction strategy.

In essence, the incorporation of a change is like a mini-project, with all the inherent variables that can alter its execution. This scenario is fertile ground on which implementation mistakes can proliferate. To illustrate this point, let's assume the following:

- Your company has 500 employees that are directly involved in developing a product.

- The product is supported by 10 vendor/suppliers.

- You are generating an average of 330 changes per month.

Given these factors, your work force could experience as many as 1,650,000 errors per month. That is 19,800,000 potential product related errors per year. This example depicts the environment wherein most new products are developed or built. It also enables one to readily discern the difficulty of maintaining effective product integrity.

However, because companies are unaware of the high probability for errors, they tend to disregard the importance of incorporation management. Instead, they merely assume that change will automatically be implemented after it has been approved. Not only is their assumption wrong, but it also precludes them from developing the intelligence systems necessary to effectively coordinate change incorporation. To better understand this intelligence need, let's examine how incorporation of a change and its *effectivity* should be managed.

CHANGE INCORPORATION VERSUS EFFECTIVITY

There are two change management terms that sound similar but have very different purposes: change *incorporation* and change *effectivity*. Incorporation is the designated *point at which* a change is planned to be implemented (e.g., date, serial number, or model number). Incorporation's purpose is to aid in planning, communicating, and coordinating the timing of a change. In contrast, effectivity is the designated *range* of a change. An effectivity defines the date, serial number, or model number *where* a change will become effective.

For example, let's say that a product change is scheduled to be *incorporated* on serial number 150, with an *effectivity* of "100 and on." Assume that you are currently producing serial number 150. This means the current production model must be reworked to the new configuration. At this point, all materials, processes, and documentation must be changed to the new configuration. Also, the change effectivity specifies that previously built products, serial numbers 100–149, must be retrofitted to meet the requirements of the change. As you can see, determining the effectivity of a change can be a costly decision. Therefore, it should be considered a business as well as a technical decision.

Critical incorporation activities do not happen without detailed planning and control. The ability to achieve this objective is based on the awareness and predictability of the coordination, integration, and communication necessary to successfully implement the change. The complexity of this task is influenced by two factors: (1) the rate of work and (2) business operating systems.

The Rate of Work

As one might imagine, the rate or flow of work is an extremely fragile planning factor. It changes frequently in most businesses. For example,

- Production engineering may complete the installation of a new process or item of capital equipment that increases or decreases the processing rate.

- A machine may be pulled off-line for extended maintenance, reducing the flow of work.

- An operator may misread a tolerance and produce an unacceptable part for a critical work order.

- Management or a customer may expedite an order that resequences the flow of work.

- A vendor's work force may announce a strike, delaying a needed shipment of parts.

These are real-life dynamics that can affect the rate of production, schedule of work, and *the point of incorporation*. So what's the big deal? you say, Welcome to life on the shop floor!

Well here's the big deal. If you produce 500 widgets a day, missing the incorporation point by only one day will result in 500 wrong widgets that might have been shipped, or need to be scrapped or reworked. Either way, you've got a problem.

Business Operating Systems

The dynamics introduced by variations in the rate of work are only part of the story. However, the previous example addressed only the difficulties involved in managing the incorporation and effectivity of one change. In reality, the average company processes nearly 4,000 changes per year!

This means that you may have several, hundreds of, or thousands of changes simultaneously in process—each change dependent on preceding or pending changes. To put this in perspective, recall how involved the simple task of rescheduling a staff meeting can be. Now multiply this effort by the number of people required to incorporate a change. Then multiply again by the number of changes you're presently experiencing.

This degree of "assimilation overload" can quickly encumber the best operating systems. More important, this environment can impede the productivity of your work force. Therefore, your business operating "systems" (people, and hardware and software) must be capable of supporting the incorporation requirements generated by your product development process.

We discussed many of these informational requirements

in Chapter Eight. However, while this type of change management system is critical for controlling change, it is only part of the communication solution. Wide-ranging user needs transcend even the best change tracking system.

User needs also encompass the capability of inventory control, scheduling, and procurement systems to accommodate effectivity points, old and new part numbers, cost differentials, and traceability of past and pending changes. More important, these requirements must be presented to a wide variety of users in a "user-friendly" way.

In one company, the change management system produced a report that indicated all approved changes. However, if one wanted to know if there were any new changes, one had to manually compare yesterday's and today's reports to locate any new incorporation requirements. Nor did the system provide visibility of pending changes to support the needs of functional planners. Without visibility of pending changes, the master scheduler might wisely try to stay ahead of demand by scheduling an order for 1,000 widgets to increase his utilization rate, satisfy a customer order, and add 500 units to inventory. Unfortunately, he wouldn't know a change was pending that would require reworking each of the 500 units just put into stock. Nor would the purchasing agent who negotiated a great price for a large order of now obsolete components. Are these normal operational problems? Perhaps, but the more obvious question is, How much could have been saved if each had only been aware of the pending change?

The message is clear. The added value of user-friendly business operating systems that meet your change management needs can greatly dwarf their development costs. Imagine the competitive advantage of minimizing the likelihood of experiencing a 1,650,000 monthly error rate!

When incorporation and effectivities are not properly managed, the integrity of the product is lost. Unfortunately, this occurs too often in too many businesses. The method most widely used to regain control is to compare the *physical* "as-built" product to the *documented* "as-planned" product to ensure that all changes have been made.

While this approach may achieve ultimate, or final, product integrity, it does little to prevent the tragic Western profile depicted in the Japanese/Western comparative model (see Chapter Four). This approach of auditing the product to correct the paperwork is as outdated as yesterday's quality inspector, who sat at the end of the production line and accepted or rejected the final product. The results of the quality revolution have proved that relying on feedback from final inspection was too late and too expensive, and provided too little problem solving value.

We now realize that quality must be built into the product. A similar economy of time and cost applies when change is planned correctly and incorporated properly. Product integrity must be built into the product development process. An effective change incorporation methodology is the key to operationalizing this critical product development success factor.

ANALYZING YOUR INCORPORATION PROCESS

The wellness of an incorporation process is the most difficult product development management principle to analyze. This is because most businesses do not track the necessary incorporation information. Nevertheless, you cannot afford not to begin. There are three steps to this analysis: determining the magnitude of the problem, controlling the incorporation of approved product changes, and determining potential cost savings.

Step 1: Determine the Magnitude of the Problem

In Chapter Eight, Effectively Managing Product Change, we discussed how the frequency and rate of change can model whether change management is an issue requiring corrective action. However, while this analysis can reveal the magnitude and periodicity of change, it will not identify incorporation problems that are incurred after a change has been approved. These costs can only be determined by evaluating your processes to plan, track, "replan," and confirm the incorporation of change.

The following key questions can guide your investigation:

- How are incorporation dates planned and integrated for approved changes?

- How accurate is this information?

- How many approved changes require support from manufacturing, engineering, materials, or other functional element?

- How many approved changes require support from outside vendors or subcontractors?

- Do your business operating systems support change incorporation requirements?

- When was the last audit to ensure that changes were incorporated as planned?

- Who manages the change incorporation tracking system?

- Is there a process for replanning a change if the approved incorporation point cannot be achieved?

- Who is empowered to authorize replanning of an

approved change that cannot be accomplished as planned?

- Does the tracking system provide the following information: (1) Task, schedule, and responsibility of each functional recipient? (2) Planned and actual start and completion dates by function? and (3) Estimated and actual budgeted material and man-hour costs by function?

- How many approved changes are incorporated on their planned incorporation date?

- How many approved changes are past their planned incorporation date?

- How many changes have been replanned in the past one, three, or six months?

The answers to the above questions can help you understand and visualize the full impact of change on your functional resources, their productivity, and your product costs. For example, when a high-tech office equipment manufacturer was confronted with competitive pressures, the CEO sought ways to cut product costs by 30 percent. His initial plan was to move the manufacturing effort to an offshore facility to trim labor costs. By so doing, he opted for the traditional "POP" method of reducing costs—getting "people off the payroll." However, further investigation revealed that the company's total labor costs to produce the product were less than 8 percent. Eliminating all labor costs would not have achieved his target! However, the CEO's ineffective change management process revealed a significant savings opportunity. He learned that virtually every product change request was approved as soon as it was requested. No attempt was made to screen these requests or plan the most cost-effective point of incorporation.

To his surprise, the CEO also learned that he could reduce his product cost by nearly 27 percent by simply planning, scheduling, and incorporating product change more effectively! Like most managers, he had failed to grasp the cost of accommodating a high degree of change activity in an already complex product development environment. Nor did he appreciate the skills his functional "doers" needed to assimilate how these cumulative changes affected their respective work. Moving manufacturing operations out of country without successfully addressing the question of change management would have only exacerbated the situation.

Step 2: Control the Incorporation of Approved Product Changes

Effective change incorporation requires a "closed-loop" system to track and control a change from the time it is approved until it is satisfactorily incorporated by each required functional element. However, because most companies do not manage a change after it has been approved, incorporation breaks down very rapidly. As a result, timely communication of change requirements does not occur.

Unattainable incorporation schedules are seldom rescheduled. This integration and coordination breakdown destroys product integrity, debilitates functional efficiency, and adds unnecessary product costs. For example, procurement may needlessly incur expediting fees to support a change without knowing that its incorporation will be delayed because engineering will be unable to achieve their schedule. Without an adequate change tracking system, there will be no feedback to engineering and management concerning the true status and cost of design change. This feedback is as essential to organizational learning as coaching is to an athlete. Without it, you will continue doing what you've always done and getting the results you've always gotten.

Step 3: Determine Potential Cost Savings

The costs of administratively processing change are only a small portion of the change cost equation. The most significant costs result from the incorporation of change: designing the "fix," reworking completed products, dispositioning scrap, expediting suppliers, determining schedule impacts, obsoleting material, overcoming lost sales opportunities, performing warranty and repair work, preventing erosion of customer satisfaction, and implementing process and procedural changes.

The cost of incorporation is typically four to six times greater than a change's administrative processing cost. Assuming that you are experiencing the average number of product changes discussed in Chapter Four, your monthly costs could be as follows.

Changes Per Month	Incorporation Costs ($ millions)*		
	× 4	× 5	× 6
330	$18.4	$23.0	$27.6
1,000	$56.0	$70.0	$84.0

*Assumes $1,400 administrative cost per change (e.g., 330 × $1,400 × 4 = $18.4).

Another significant benefit of effective incorporation management is the elimination of the need to conduct "as-built" versus "as-planned" product inspections. Other potential cost savings can be calculated by evaluating

• The cost of accommodating "product returns"

because an approved change had not been correctly incorporated.

- The cost of retrofitting products in the field.
- The cost of product recalls.
- The cost of dealer repairs.
- The loss of key customers or market share because of perceived lack of product integrity, lack of reliability, or failure.

Managing the incorporation of change is an internally controllable means to significantly improve your competitiveness for several reasons. First, complete your analysis and calculate the potential benefits that could be derived and then visualize the millions of profit contribution dollars—if you could save only 25 percent of your incorporation costs! Second, enhancing the integrity of your products is an absolute requirement to sustain the product development requirements mandated by international initiatives such as ISO 9000.

PDM: AN INTERNATIONAL ISSUE

There is another compelling reason why you should take immediate action to assure the integrity, stability, and predictability of your product development process: *Unless you can effectively operationalize these principles, you may be locked out of international or global markets.* The reason for this challenge to your survivability is an international quality initiative of escalating importance: ISO 9000.

ISO 9000 is rapidly becoming the accepted international quality standard for virtually every industrialized country in the world. The basic premise of this binding agreement is beginning in 1992, signatories of the standard will give purchase preference to ISO 9000 certified companies. In short, if you plan to sell to international or global markets you must comply with the provisions of ISO 9000.

The International Standards Organization's (ISO's) definition of quality is a simple one: fitness for purpose. This interpretation does not imply a specific "faults per million" or "six-sigma" type of quality criteria. Instead, ISO 9000 states that a product's "fitness" is an issue to be decided between the buyer and the seller.

The only demand placed on this arrangement is that the seller must have a *verified* process in place to ensure that each product or service delivered to the buyer will equal the preceding ones. Sounds like the role of product integrity, doesn't it? In essence, ISO 9000 *mandates that the integrity of a seller's products or services must be verified by an independent auditor.*

The implications of this statement are twofold. First, the initiatives that enable product development integrity must be implemented and operational *before* they can be audited and verified. Second, observed and measurable results must precede verification. Furthermore, the independent auditor must be certified and registered by the ISO committee. What do these requirements mean to you? If you haven't already begun ISO 9000 verification, you're probably 12–18 months from certification and 12–18 months from international product acceptability.

While these commonsense standards might seem like Introduction to Business 101, their impact on corporate wellness could be devastating. Failure to comply with ISO 9000 can literally block all future international sales opportunities. Therefore, it is important to understand the compliance requirements of the three basic ISO 9000 standards:

- ISO 9001 applies to companies involved in complete product development. This encompasses design, development, and manufacture through after-sale repair and service. This initiative most appropriately addresses the typical product development scenario.

- ISO 9002 applies to companies involved only in the manufacture, test, final inspection, and installation of a product. ISO 9002 assumes that the design and development of a product are accomplished by an entity separate from the manufacturer.

- ISO 9003 applies to companies involved only in the test and final inspection of a product.

There are several major differences between ISO 9000 and other quality initiatives. The most obvious is that ISO 9000 encompasses the entire product development and commercialization effort—from marketing, to design, to vendors, to quality assurance, to executive management—not just the manufacturing processes. Another significant difference is that the application criteria are unambiguous. They leave little room for interpretation. You are either in one category or another. For example, if your company designs, develops, produces, tests, installs, or assembles the product and then continues to provide for its service, you must comply with ISO 9001.

ISO 9000 and Effective Product Development

Once you understand the strategic intent of ISO 9000, you can visualize the foundational values this initiative can instill within a product development process. It also enables you to visualize the importance of operationalizing a capability to

- Verify and control a design to assure that it meets customer requirements.

- Provide employees with correct product documentation at all times.

- Assure stability and control of product development processes.

- Maintain an effective incoming, in-process, and final product quality management system.

- Calibrate test equipment to ensure correct measurement of tolerances.

- Certify vendors as appropriate.

- Maintain appropriate product records and documentation.

Another significant factor of these ISO initiatives is the ISO committee's registered third-party certification requirement. It is the role of this audit team, not the manufacturer, to determine whether a product equals the sum of its definition, system requirements, manufacturing practices, and processes—throughout the development and production process.

A Reason for Change

If your company is like most, you probably have not been aware of the need for and benefits of effective incorporation of change. Therefore, it will take ingenuity to validate the status of your change incorporation process. This can cause a bittersweet scenario—*bitter* because there often is so little documentation that it is difficult (without intuitive deduction) to calculate the real value of effective change incorporation and *sweet* because there may also be much fertile ground for improvement.

One CEO had a unique way of comparing his company's flawed management of change to his early days as a young farmer. "Have you ever shoveled manure?" he asked. "Remember how that first shovelful took your breath away? Then, by the time the spreader was full, you could sit on top of the pile and eat your lunch. Well, that is about where we are."

Regrettably, this is where many businesses also find themselves—sitting on top of the pile. They've become accustomed to the stench of waste and confusion of uncontrolled change. Even worse, they've adopted ways to institutionalize it. Fortunately, you've been made aware of the need for, and the path toward, change. You've been made aware that your competitive success may rely on two factors. First, you must responsively introduce ways to achieve greater product development integrity. Second, and perhaps more important, you must lead your organization's efforts to operationalize these initiatives. Your future global revenues will depend upon your success.

Chapter Ten

Energizing Your Organization for Action

The discussions in the preceding chapters were intended to inform, guide, and challenge your thoughts toward a new product development paradigm. As such, these discussions have bridged current "strategic business think" with competitive business scenarios of the future. They've contrasted Eastern and Western management methodologies.

Avant-garde approaches have been innovatively forged from proven down-to-earth principles. Now the time for discussion and contemplation is over. It is time for you to internalize the concepts and principles presented. It is time for you to analyze your product development management effectiveness. It is time for you to evaluate the potential of these concepts and principles for improving your product development processes. And it is time for you to operationalize opportunities for saving costs, time, and other critical resources.

Insights generated from business interventions and practical examples have been distilled and crystallized into proven product development management principles. The case examples have shown how implementation of these principles can save you millions of dollars per year while significantly improving your product development performance. Hopefully, this book has compelled you to change—to move toward a paradigm of greater competitiveness.

However, the *need* to change and the *ability* to change are two very different issues. The key question is not, Do you need to make these major operational changes? The arguments against maintaining the status quo are too overwhelming to ignore. No, the more pertinent question is, Can you make them in time?

This assertion is not intended to be condescending by any means. It is merely an acknowledgment that successful implementation of major organizational change is typically plagued by barriers. Overcoming these barriers requires a combination of science and art.

BARRIERS TO CHANGE

Change and human nature are like oil and water—neither mixes well. It is our human nature to resist change. We each want to do things our way. We all want others to get in step with our drumbeat.

Businesses act in much the same manner with one major exception: the intrigues of business. The intrigues of the corporate environment amplify our natural resistance to change. Indeed, the perceived implications of change on prestige, security, and business equilibrium can quickly raise our level of resistance from nuisance to insecurity to fear.

While change may seem unnatural, it is nature that provides a simple analogy to guide us. Just as the four seasons change from one to another in a logical pattern, so does behavioral change follow a logical process. Physics also offers four natural laws of change:

- Inertia: "*I* don't want to change."
- Mass: "*We* don't want to change."
- Force: "*You* will change!"
- Acceleration: "And quickly!"

However, if you wish to prevent or overcome the fear of change, you first need to discern its source. In turn, overcoming the fear of change minimizes the barriers to change. The five most dominant barriers are the following:

1. *Invincibility.* Invincibility is one of the greatest sources of corporate arrogance. We are so often blinded by our past that we fail to recognize the need for change. In fact, the bigger and more successful we are, the more difficult it will be to change. The automobile industry provides a classic example of this blindness. For too long, carmakers held to their belief that what was good for Detroit was good for the customer. They didn't perceive the need for change until their invincibility was repeatedly confronted by an eroding market share to the Japanese.

2. *Institutionalization.* Institutionalization is not only a big word but a big barrier as well. It means that we have developed, documented, trained, rewarded, and inculcated certain practices and behaviors over time. The threat of *changing* these practices alters the very stability this "bureaucratic security" provides.

3. *Functionalization.* Functionalization introduces a number of issues into the corporate environment. Unfortunately, few are positive. Most of these concern politics, empire building, suboptimization, parochialism, and a general lack of empathy and understanding for those beyond functional walls. This typically causes more turf battles to be fought within corporate walls than on inner-city streets.

4. *The magnitude of the task.* Change fails to occur when its true magnitude is not fully understood. Perhaps this is because of our atomistic programming. It's often easier to concentrate on the bits rather than focusing on the whole. However, an insightful business leader must see beyond the portended results of these atomistic initiatives. The successful agent of change must be able to visualize and discern the breadth of change. Understanding the "mass" of change is essential to creating a plan to achieve it.

5. *The lack of a common vision.* This barrier poses a dilemma for most companies. On one hand, significant organizational change cannot be successful where common visions do not exist. On the other, each person views the business through his or her own personal "knothole." Therefore, before change can begin, a critical mass of people must understand and accept your vision. This is the reason why change by edict or memo is seldom effective. To be successful, both the innovator and the executor—the CEO and the union worker on the assembly line—must share a common need *for* and a common vision *of* the change.

THE CHANGE PROCESS: OVERCOMING CHANGE BARRIERS

What is most often overlooked in attempting change is that it affects one critical element: people. Human group dynamics are always a much greater barrier to change than is technological complexity. Mastering change demands that businesses become more effective in dealing with the people side of organization change.

Successful change evolves through a logical four-phase process. The phases are unawareness, awareness, vision, and operationalization.

Phase 1: Unawareness

Unawareness is akin to inertia—nothing is happening. Although the need to change may exist, the need is not perceived. Being unaware is like living in a world without mirrors. One can see the beauty or flaws in others, but not in oneself.

Similarly, functional elements can more easily see problems in everyone other than themselves. This gives rise to corporate fiefdoms, parochialism, and suboptimized functional perspectives. Unless the state of unawareness can be broken, change will not occur.

Phase 2: Awareness

Awareness is the trigger point in the change process. It occurs when the need for change is recognized and internalized. An overweight person, for example, becomes painfully aware of the need to diet by seeing his or her profile in a mirror.

Organizations are as reluctant to change as individuals are. Countering this resistance requires development of "organizational mirrors" as the precursor to change. A designer may not be motivated to change behavior until the number and costs of his or her design errors are "mirrored" back to them in the form of a performance feedback vehicle. The purpose of these mirrors is to provide a means for the viewer to assimilate and interpret, to "see" and internalize the need for change.

Phase 3: The Vision

Changing *from* something assumes changing *to* something else. This implies that you define *where you are* and *where you need to go* before launching a significant change project. During the 1980 presidential election campaign, George Bush chided Ronald Reagan about his "vision thing." Political pundits maintain that President Bush lost the 1992 election in part to Bill Clinton's ability to articulate a clearer vision for America. The vision facilitates the operationalization of change by

- Defining the path forward and providing a means of measuring the success of the journey.
- Stating the *why* as well as the *what* of the proposed change.
- Identifying and integrating the need for training; organizational realignment; and definition of new responsibilities, policies, and procedures.

Phase 4: Operationalization

Of the four phases of change, the operationalization phase is the most demanding, most time-consuming, most costly, and most often underestimated part of the change process. Operationalization is where the management team, individuals, and work groups develop and implement the new methods and procedures. More important, it is the phase where the management team, individuals, and work groups train, internalize, and routinely begin to follow these new methods and procedures.

Your Leadership Role

Executive management's active and visible participation is a critical element in successfully implementing change.

The greater the "mass" to overcome, the more truer this statement becomes. Major organizational changes, such as those required to operationalize the new product development paradigm, fit this mold. Such changes involve virtually every function and element of your business. They raise sensitive business and human planning issues that cannot be delegated. History has shown that determined military leaders can change the momentum of a battle through visible personal leadership. Business leaders must do the same.

Make no mistake. In the ever escalating battle for competitiveness, your competitors are not standing still. All cannot be successful, and their continued success is your continued loss.

THE NEW PARADIGM AND THE CHANGE PROCESS

Using the modified precepts of Sun Tzu as a guide, let's integrate the principles of the new paradigm and the change process to energize your organization to successfully achieve it.

Step 1: Where Are You in the Change Continuum?

Change will not begin until the need for change is known. Therefore, a starting point is to quantitatively define why you need to change. This could take the form of declining revenues, market share, or profit margins; increasing competition in technology; inability to introduce new products on time; the need to improve quality and reliability; or pressure to reduce costs. Or it could be a simple directive from corporate headquarters that increases your profit contribution requirements for the coming year.

The point to remember is that you must quantitatively

show why change is imperative. More important, how will this change affect each organizational element? What's in it for me? is a very real question your people will ask. You must provide the answers.

Step 2: "Mirroring" the Need to Change

We know that the successful implementation of change requires an awareness of the *need* to change. In essence, you must create mirrors that reflect reality in ways that can enable each employee to visualize why he or she needs to change. Since the genesis of the new product development paradigm begins at the customer/business interface, isn't it logical that this is where the first mirror should be built? For example, you may want to measure the following:

- Whether you really know your customers, their needs and wants, and their perceived product attribute values.

- Whether you are able to correctly identify and evaluate new product ideas.

- Whether you are gaining or losing customers, market share, or profit contribution. If you are losing, to whom and why?

- Whether your product development cycle supports your customer/competitive requirements.

- Whether your customers are more or less satisfied with your product price, performance, and services. If not, why not? If so, why?

Greater awareness can also enable you to identify whether your product development strategy is focused *from* the customer or *toward* the customer. This awareness can be simultaneously developed in several mutually supporting areas by following the following four product development management principles:

(1) *Product definition.* Develop a periodicity model (refer back to Figure 8–2) and compare this model with the Japanese/Western comparative model (refer back to Figure 2–1). This will provide a visual snapshot of how well your product definition process is performing. If your analysis warrants, continue to explore the product definition issues discussed in Chapters Seven and Eight.

(2) *Definition control.* Evaluate your product development process to determine whether it is actually being used and where specific work flow problems exist, and identify recommendations for improvement. Also determine how a new product is defined, reviewed, and approved. More important, how is this definition controlled as it is being communicated and translated by the functional elements?

(3) *Change control.* Change is one of the best indications of a broken product development process. When a product's definition is not adequately defined or controlled, changes proliferate to accommodate for lack of understanding, coordination, or communication. Capture these change dynamics and calculate their costs and schedule impacts. This is a major awareness mirror for most organizations.

(4) *Incorporation.* Incorporation is the operationalization of change. As such, it is usually more complex, uncontrolled, and costly than the change approval process. Therefore, if change control

indicated a problem, expect that problem to be four to six times greater in the areas of incorporation.

Step 3: Developing and Operationalizing the Vision

While awareness mirrors reflect *where you are*, the vision defines *where you need to go*. This means that you must also guide and integrate the planning, training, documentation, systems development, procedures, policies, reengineering, realignment of roles and responsibilities, and increased communications necessary to get there. Although this is perhaps the most difficult phase of change, it is the role of business leadership to create the awareness, discern the vision, and orchestrate a path forward.

This book is your guide to achieving the new paradigm. Chapters Two, Three and Four provide a unique and holistic overview of the product development process. Chapters Five and Six discuss the new product development paradigm and the principles, methodologies, and steps to achieve it.

Chapters Seven, Eight, and Nine explore its possibilities, processes, and opportunities. Analysis techniques have been included to help you evaluate the need for change and determine the benefits of doing so. Together they can assist you to define a holistic vision for achieving a more competitive and harmoniously integrated business.

THE QUEST FOR COMPETITIVENESS

This book is about the business of business. It is about competitiveness. It is about new product development. More specifically, it is about the need for a new product development paradigm.

In this regard, the new paradigm, being a theoretical

pattern or a collective framework of thought, does not necessarily represent more knowledge than the old one, but rather a *new perspective*.[33] When a critical number of people accept a new idea, a collective paradigm shift occurs.

I submit that the new product development paradigm shift has occurred. Unfortunately, indicators suggest it is not yet occurring within Western businesses with sufficient critical mass to offset foreign competitive threats. This is a message that has been difficult to deliver to Western business leaders for several reasons.

First, negative news is seldom delivered because it is seldom accepted. Second, the strategies and visions of a business are often intertwined with the leadership's or the organization's identities. Third, the proverbial messengers of bad news do not wish to be shot!

This is not "new" news. Bacon and Voltaire were painfully conscious of these pressures as they wrote their historical accounts. "If they were to survive, they knew they must not offend those in charge. For these writers, history was at best a compromise, full of codes and ciphers to protect not only the authors, but their messages."[34]

These codes and ciphers still exist in every business environment. The principles and perspectives in this book can enable you to discern, understand, and decode these heretofore uncipherable ciphers. Yet for all its promise, the quest for competitiveness can only begin when you are able to develop and introduce new products faster, more reliably, and at less cost than your competitors. The quest for competitiveness can only begin when you are better at making and selling than anyone else. The quest for competitiveness can only begin when you are able to operationalize a new product development paradigm that is right for your business. The quest for competitiveness can only begin when you are ready to lead the way to the change.

Endnotes

Preface

1. Oren Harari, "Cars, Customers & Competition: Lessons for American Managers," *Management Review*, February 1991, p. 40.

Chapter 1

2. Jeffrey G. Miller and Jay S. Kim, "Beyond the Quality Revolution: U.S. Manufacturing Strategy in the 1990s," *Manufacturing Roundtable*, Boston University, 1990, p. 11.

3. Ibid., p. 16.

4. Philip H. Francis, "Editorial," *Manufacturing Review* 3, no. 4 (December 1990), p. 215.

5. John H. Sheridan, "Productivity Sags," *Industry Week*, November 1990, p. 60.

6. Steven Schlosstein, "Pax Nipponica: The Era of Japan's Dominance?" *Engineering Management Review*, December 1990, p. 105.

7. John A. Adams, "Industries Transcend National Boundaries," *IEEE Spectrum*, September 1990, p. 26.

8. Steven Schlossstein, "Pax Nipponica."

9. Jim Impoco, "The United States and Japan Are Competing Role Models," *U.S. News and World Report*, December 30, 1991–January 6, 1992, p. 50.

10. Steven Schlossstein, "Pax Nipponica."

11. Impoco, "The United States and Japan."

12. "About the ISO 9000/Q90 Standards," *On Q Newsletter* VII, no. 9 (November 1992), p. 4.

13. "U.S. Manufacturers Slow to Gain ISO 9000 Certification," *On Q Newsletter* VII, no. 9 (November 1992), p. 4.

14. Impoco, "The United States and Japan."

15. Samuel B. Griffith, *The Art of War*, Sun Tzu, p. 84. Oxford University Press, New York 1963.

Chapter 2

16. Dean Black, Ph.D., "China's Ancient Gift to Modern Quest for Health," *Regeneration*, p. 2. 1988 by Bioresearch Foundation.

17. Gerald M. Hoffman, "Small Resources, Big Results," *Information Management Forum*, American Management Association, January 1991, p. 1.

18. Kim B. Clark, and Takahiro Fujimoto, "The Power of Product Integrity," *Harvard Business Review*, November–December 1990, p. 110.

19. L.P. Sullivan, "Quality Function Deployment," *Quality Progress*, June 1986, p. 39.

Chapter 3

20. George Ohsawa, *The Art of Peace* (Oroville, Calif.: Macrobiotic Foundation, 1952), Chap. 12.

21. Jearl Walker, "The Amateur Scientist," *Scientific American*, January 1988, p. 97.

Chapter 4

22. R. G. Cooper, and E. J. Kleinschmidt, "Resource Allocation in the New Product Process," *Industrial Marketing Management* 17 (1988), p. 260.

23. Cooper and Kleinschmidt, "Resource Allocation."

24. Ibid.

25. Julia King, "Life in the Slow Lane," *Computer-World*, February 3, 1992, p. 67.

Chapter 5

26. James Daly, "Apple's Corporate Campaign Fights Counterculture Past," September 16, 1991, p. 6.

27. Mark Landler, "Mercedes Finds Out How Much Is Too Much," *Business Week*, January 20, 1992, p. 92.

28. David M. Reid, "Where Planning Fails in Practice," *Long Range Planning* 23, no. 2 (1990), p. 87.

29. Cooper and Kleinschmidt, "Resource Allocation."

Chapter 6

30. Brian Dumain, "Earning More by Moving Faster," *Fortune*, October 7, 1991, p. 94.

31. Dumain, "Earning More."

Chapter 7

32. Brian Dumain, "Earning More by Moving Faster," *Fortune*, October 7, 1991, p. 94.

Chapter 10

33. Robert Hieronimus, Ph.D., "The Amerindian Influence on the Founders' Vision," *America's Secret Destiny* (Rochester, Vt.: Destiny Books, 1989), p. 5.

34. Hieronimus, "The New Age and the Great Seal," *America's Secret Destiny* (Rochester, Vt.: Destiny Books, 1989), p. 63.

Index

A

Actioning and communicating change requests, 133–34
Actual versus estimated cost report on change, 142
Actual versus estimated schedule report on change, 143
Aging report, on change, 142
Apple Computer, 58
Approved product changes and change incorporation, control of, 154–55
Art of visualization, 28–30
Art of War (Sun Tzu), 10
Atomism/vitalism
  and competition, 27
  and Eastern/Western management and product development styles, 20–25
  and Japanese approach, 24–26
  Musubi and, 28–37
  origin of terms, 20
  U.S. approach, 26–27

Audit, material kit issues, 120–22
Average change processing time report, 142
Awareness of need to change, 165

B

Balance, 30–32
Barriers to change, product development process, 162–64
  overcoming barriers, 164–67
Bottom-up product development, 21–22
Bush, George, 166
Business operating systems, and product integrity, 149–51
Business/product intelligence, and product change, 130–33

C

Change administration versus change management, 124–27

Change control, 169
Change control board (CCB), 135–39
Change incorporation, 147
  versus effectivity, 147–51
Change management compression, 136–39
Change management operating system evaluation, 140–43
Change process expediting, 134–35
Change request reduction, 128
Change requests screening, 127–30
Change request to change order conversion, 142
Changes process analysis, 126–27
Channeling creativity, product development, 80
Chi, 20
Chrysler, 39
Clinton, Bill, 166
Coleman Corporation, 81, 89
Common vision lack, as barrier to change, 164
Communicating product's definition, 73–76
Competitive forces, and product development, 3–8
Competitive renaissance, need for, 8–10
Competitors, knowledge of, and product development, 12
Comprehendibileness, and product definition, 93–94
Comprehensiveness, and product definition, 92–93
Continuous improvement (CI), product change management myth, 117–19
Conway, W. E., 70
Cost containment, product development, 52–54
Cost management, product change management, 139–40
Cost of change by function report, 143
Cost reduction, as reason for product change, 132
Customer/business interface, 63–64, 85

Customer requests, as source of and reason for product change, 131–32
Cycle of product development, 48–50

D

Decision process, effective, 81–82
Decisive engagement, product development and, 17–18
Definition control, product development process, 169
Democritus, 20
Dependent and independent design zones, product development process, 103–8
Design changes, 44–46, 47–48, 51–52
Design freezing, 114–17
Design-it-as-we-go approach, 45
Developer's perspective, 78–79
Developing and operationalizing vision, 170
Disruptive effects reduction, change requests, 128–30
Drucker, Peter, 68

E

Early and customer-focused product definition, 61–68
Eastern approach, product development, 20–26
Effective decision process, product development management, 81–82
Effective product development defined, 1
80/20 rule, 104–5
Engineering requests, and product change, 131
European Community (EC), as product development competition, 4–6, 42
Evaluating product change management, 140–43
Expediting product change, 134–35

F

Farmer, Mike, 89
Formal approval, product definition, 95–96
Freezing design, product change management myth, 114–17
Functionalization, as barrier to change, 163–64
Fuzzy companies, 74–76

G

General Motors, 39

H

Harmonious unification, 32–35
Hippocrates, 20
Holistic approach. *See* Atomism/ vitalism
Honda, 22
Horace, 18
"Hurry-up" approach, product design and development, 108–10

I

IBM, 39
Incorporating changes, 169–70
Incorporation process analysis, 151–56
Independent design zones establishment, 106–8
Industrial revolution, 38
Institutionalization, as barrier to change, 163
Institutionalized product development inadequacies, 54–55
Integrating versus intellectualizing, 32–34
Integrator's challenge, 86
International standards for product development, 7–8

International Standards Organization (ISO) requirements, 7–8, 156–58
Invincibility, as barrier to change, 163

J

Jackson, Michael J., 58
Japanese/Western comparison model
achieving product reliability, maintainability, and quality targets, 50–52
design changes, 52, 55
and new paradigm, 85
plateaus of stability, 45–48
product definition timing, 42–45
product development cost containment, 52–56
stability and cycle comparison opportunities, 48–50
Japan/Japanese
economic success of, 19
product development cycle in, 55
timing of product definition, 43
and vitalistic approach, management and product development, 24–26

L

Late and inwardly focused product definition, 59–61
Leadership role in change, 166–67
Lincoln, Abraham, 16

M

McDonald's, 145
Make-to-work, as reason for product change, 132
Malcolm Baldrige award, 68

Manufacturing methodologies, programs for, 38–39
Manufacturing requests, and product change, 131–32
Material kit issues, audit of, 120–22
Materials requests, and product change, 131
Mercedes Benz, 58
Mexico, as product development competition, 6–7
"Mirroring" need to change, 168–70
Musubi, principles of, 12
   art of visualization, 28–30
   balance, 30–32
   examples of, 28–29
   harmonious unification, 32–25
   oneness, 35–37
Myths, product change management, 114–20

N

Nature of work, 39–42
New product opportunities, old paradigm, 59

O

Oneness, 35–37
Operationalization, as phase of change, 166
Operational problems, 45–48
Operational turbulence, 46
Optimum staffing approach, product design and development, 110–11
Organizational elements management, product development, 84–86
Organizational learning, change management and, 143
Organizational stability and product development process, 100–101

P

Perceived customer value, 65–67
Periodicity profile, and change management, 122–24
Perodicity model, product definition, 169
Philosophic approaches. *See* Atomism/vitalism
Place on change continuum, 167–68
Plateaus of stability, and product definition, 45–48
"POP" method of cost reduction, 153
Potential cost savings, and change incorporation, 155–56
Precise and decisive action, and product development, 16–17
Principles and process integration, product development, 82–84
Principles of product development management, 71–73
Problem magnitude, and change incorporation, 152–54
Problems concerning product development, 2–3
Process, product development, 76–74
Processing time reduction, change requests, 130
Process stability assurance
   building stability into product development process, 101–102
   dependent and independent design zones, 103–6
   "hurry-up" approach, 108–10
   independent design zones establishment, 106–8
   optimum staffing approach, 110–11
   organizational stability and product development process, 100–101
   product definition process, 90–96
   and product development management, 111–12
   rationalizing product definition, 98–100

Process stability assurance—
      Cont.
   source of stability, 88–90
   stability maintainance, 102–3
   validating product definition,
      96–98
Producer's perspective, 79
Producibility, as reason for
      product change, 132
Product attributes, 64–65
Product change management
   actioning and communicating
      change requests, 133–34
   business/product intelligence,
      130–33
   change process analysis, 126–27
   change request screening, 127–
      30
   compressing, 136–39
   continuous improvement, 117–
      20
   cost management of, 139–40
   elements of, 135–39
   evaluating, 140–43
   expediting change process, 134–
      35
   freezing design, 114–17
   managing versus administering
      change, 124–27, 134
   myths concerning, 114–20
   and organizational learning, 143
   periodicity profile, 122–24
   temperature check (material kit
      issue audit), 120–22
Product definition
   change in strategy and tactics,
      70–71
   communicating, 73–76
   customer/business interface, 63–
      64
   in Japan, 43
   nature of work, 39–42
   new paradigm: early and
      customer focused, 61–68
   perceived customer value, 65–67
   periodicity model, 169
   and plateaus of stability, 45–48
   process of, 90–96
   product attributes, 64–65
   and product development costs,
      52–54

Product definition—*Cont.*
   and product reliability,
      maintainability, and quality
      targets, 50–52
   protectionist strategy, 60–61
   rationalization of, 98–100
   selling versus making, 67–68
   stability and cycle compression
      opportunities, 48–50
   timing of, 42–25
   today's paradigm: late and
      inwardly focused, 57–61
   validation of, 96–98
   Western approach to, 43–45
Product definition process, 90–96
Product development
   barriers to change in process of,
      162–64
   change process, steps in,
      167–70
   competitive forces and, 3–7
   competitive renaissance, need
      for, 8–11
   containing costs of, 52–54
   cycle of, 48–50
   decisive engagement, need for,
      17–18
   Eastern approach to, 20–26
   effective product development
      defined, 1
   and European Community,
      4–5
   institutionalized inadequacies
      in, 54–56
   international standards for,
      7–8
   International Standards
      Organization (ISO), 7–8,
      156–59
   Japanese approach to, 24–26
   leadership role in, 166–67
   phases of change in process of,
      164–67
   problems concerning, 2–3
   and quest for competitiveness,
      170–71
   strategy for, 10–11
   tenants of effective, 11–17
   U.S. approach to, 26–27
   Western approach to, 21–22, 26–
      27

Product development capability,
knowledge of, 13–16
Product development costs,
52–54
Product development management
(PDM)
channeling creativity, 80
communicating product
definition, 73–76
defined, 69–70
developer's perspective, 78–79
developmental structure,
77–78
development process, 76–84
effective decision process,
81–82
fuzzy companies, 74–76
integrator's challenge, 86
as international issue, 156–60
organizational elements
management, 84–86
principles and process
integration, 82–84
principles of, 71–73
and process stability, 111–12
producer's perspective, 79
product integrity and,
156–60
Product development process, and
harmonious unification,
34–35
Product enhancement, as reason
for product change, 132
Product integrity
and business operating systems,
149–51
change incorporation, 146–47
change incorporation versus
effectivity, 147–51
and customer satisfaction, 144–
45
defined, 144
incorporation process analysis,
151–56
and product development
management, 156–60
rate of work, as planning factor,
148–49
Productivity improvement, means
of achieving, 38–40
Productivity influencers, 40–42

Product reliability, maintainability,
and quality targets, 50–52
Product safety, as reasons for
product change, 132
Protectionist product
development, 60–61

Q

Quality revolution, 38
Quantity of change report, 142
Quest for competitiveness,
170–71

R

Rate of work, as planning factor,
148–49
Rationalization, product
definition, 98–100
Reagan, Ronald, 166
Reengineering, 38
Return on investment (ROI)
expected, and product
change, 133

S

Sales and market requests, and
product change, 131
Sculley, John, 58
Selling versus making, 67–68
South America, as product
development competition, 7
Southeast Asia, as product
development competition, 6
Stability, and product
development process, 101–2
Stability maintainance, product
development, 102–3
Structure, product development,
77–78
Sun Tzu, 10–11, 17, 167
System engineering, independent
design zones, 106–8

T

Task magnitude, as barrier to
    change, 164
Technical review board (TRB), 138
Temperature check, and product
    change management, 120–21
Tenants of effective product
    development, 11–17
Timeliness, and product
    definition, 91–92
Time-to-margin contributions,
    product development cycle,
    49–50
Time-to-volume contributions,
    product development cycle, 49
Timing of product definition, 42–
    45
Top-down product development,
    21–22

U

Unawareness of need to change,
    165

United States approach, product
    development, 26–27

V

Validation, product definition, 96–
    98
Vision, as impetus to change, 166

W

Western approach
    product definition, 43–45
    product development, 21–22,
        26–27
Wordsworth, William, 19
WYGIWYE (what you get is what
    you expect), 145
WYSIWYG (what you see is what
    you get), 145

X

Xerox, 55

MANAGEMENT OF QUALITY
Strategies to Improve Quality and the Bottom Line

Jack Hagan

Co-published by ASQC Quality Press/Business One Irwin

This nonthreatening strategic guide presents the quality improvement process as a business—and shows you how to manage it for success. You'll discover what you must do to profit from quality, avoid common quality pitfalls, maximize your time and resources, and sustain your improvement program. (210 pages) ISBN: 1-55623-924-6

GLOBAL QUALITY
A Synthesis of the World's Best Management Methods

Richard Tabor Greene

Co-published by ASQC Quality Press/Business One Irwin

This is a complete guide for managing and coordinating different quality systems simultaneously. Greene includes 20 sure-fire approaches for improving quality and remaining competitive, seven *new* total quality methods being tested in Japan, and much more! (275 pages) ISBN: 1-55623-915-7

THE CORPORATE GUIDE TO THE MALCOLM BALDRIGE NATIONAL QUALITY AWARD
New and Revised

Marion Mills Steeples
Foreword by Robert W. Galvin, Chairman of the Executive Committee, Motorola Inc.

Co-published by ASQC Quality Press/Business One Irwin

The insider's guide to the coveted quality award! Whether you plan to apply for the Baldrige Award or just want to use its guidelines to stay competitive in today's marketplace, *The Corporate Guide* shows you how. It provides the tools you can use to cut development and production costs, streamline processes, eliminate waste, enhance worker morale, and improve customer service. (430 pages) ISBN: 1-55623-957-2

Available at fine bookstores and libraries everywhere.